The

Personality

Disorders

EXPLAINED

SECOND EDITION

David J. Robinson, M.D.

Fellow, Royal College of Physicians and
Surgeons of Canada
Fellow, American Psychiatric Association

Rapid Psychler Press 🚲

Suite 374
3560 Pine Grove Ave.
Port Huron, Michigan
USA 48060

Suite 203
1673 Richmond St.
London, Ontario
Canada N6G 2N3

Toll Free Phone   888-PSY-CHLE (888-779-2453)
Toll Free Fax   888-PSY-CHLR (888-779-2457)
Outside the U.S. & Canada — Phone 519-667-2335
Outside the U.S. & Canada — Fax 519-675-0610
website   www.psychler.com
email   rapid@psychler.com

ISBN 1-894328-26-4
© 2003, Rapid Psychler Press — Second Edition, First Printing
Printed in the United States of America

All caricatures are fictitious. Any resemblance to real people, either living or deceased, is entirely coincidental (and unfortunate). The author assumes no responsibility for the consequences of diagnoses made, or treatment instituted, as a result of the contents of this book. Only qualified mental health professionals should make diagnoses.

Every effort was made to ensure that the information in this book was accurate at the time of publication. Due to the changing nature of the field of psychiatry, the reader is encouraged to consult both additional sources of information.

Dedication

This book is dedicated to:

Susan Fletcher-Keron

Acknowledgments

I am indebted to the following individuals for their unfailing support:

- Monty & Lil Robinson
- Brian Chapman
- Dean Avola
- Tom Kay
- Susan Fletcher-Keron and Randy Keron
- Dr. Donna Robinson & Dr. Robert Bauer
- Brad Groshok & Susan McFarland

I would like to thank the following people for their many helpful suggestions regarding this book:

- Tom Norry, BSc.N.
- Sandra Northcott, M.D.
- Lisa Bogue, M.D.
- Marnie Desjardins, R.N.
- Janine Robertson, M.D.
- Noel Laporte, M.D.
- Vinay Lodha, M.D.
- Martha Wilke, BSc.OT.
- Brenda Fuhrman, LL.B., BSc.N.

Rapid Psychler Press

produces books and presentation media that are:
- comprehensively researched
- well organized
- formatted for ease of use
- reasonably priced
- clinically oriented, and
- include humor that enhances education, and that neither demeans patients nor the efforts of those who treat them

Table of Contents

Chapter 1.
Introduction to
Personality Disorders

What is a Personality Disorder?

A Definition of Personality Disorder

Personality is defined as *a relatively stable and enduring set of characteristic behavioral and emotional traits*. A **personality disorder (PD)** is a variant or an extreme set of characteristics that goes beyond the range found in most people. The **American Psychiatric Association (APA)** defines a personality disorder as: *An enduring pattern of inner experience and behavior that deviates markedly from the expectations of the individual's culture, is pervasive and inflexible, has an onset in adolescence or early adulthood, is stable over time, and leads to distress or impairment.*
Source: DSM-IV-TR, 2000, p. 685

While many other definitions exist, features consistently emphasized in describing a PD are that it:
• Is deeply ingrained and has an inflexible nature
• Is maladaptive, especially in interpersonal contexts
• Is relatively stable over time
• Significantly impairs the ability of the person to function
• Distresses those who are close to the person

PDs are enduring patterns of perceiving, thinking, feeling, and behaving that remain consistent through the majority of social situations (see p.15). Personality disorders are **egosyntonic**, meaning that an individual is not distressed by his or her behaviors. Instead, people who interact with such individuals feel the impact of the maladaptive behaviors.

Understanding Personality Disorders

One of the challenges facing clinicians and researchers who focus on PDs is that behaviors or personality characteristics do not translate readily into numbers. A medical patient is clearly hyponatremic if his sodium level falls below a certain value that that has been established by a laboratory. Similarly, a bone broken into two parts is a clear sign that the patient has a fracture. Unfortunately, personality disorders aren't diagnosed as clearly or as readily as are medical conditions.

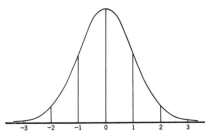

One way of understanding PDs is to consider a normal curve. The area between -2 and 2 standard deviations accounts for just over 95% of the curve. If we translate this into a human behavior, say road rage, then the concept of a PD becomes clearer. If we recorded the reactions of 100 people who are cutoff abruptly in traffic, a range of responses is likely to be observed:

• No reaction at all. . . . . Too passive

• Grips steering wheel more tightly ⎫
• Honks horn   ⎬ These are more
• Speeds by offending car   ⎪ reasonable
• Yells at other driver   ⎭ reactions

• Smashes into other car. . . . . Too aggressive

People with PDs are found at the extremes of these behaviors, which can be though of as the areas beyond -2 or 2 standard deviations on a normal curve.

The Personality Disorders

Cluster A — "Odd/Eccentric"
• Schizoid Personality Disorder (SzdPD)
• Paranoid Personality Disorder (PPD)
• Schizotypal Personality Disorder (SztPD)

Cluster B — "Dramatic/Erratic"
• Histrionic Personality Disorder (HPD)
• Antisocial Personality Disorder (ASPD)
• Borderline Personality Disorder (BPD)
• Narcissistic Personality Disorder (NPD)

Cluster C — "Anxious/Fearful"
• Avoidant Personality Disorder (APD)
• Dependent Personality Disorder (DPD)
• Obsessive-Compulsive Personality Disorder (OCPD)

Diagnostic Points

The **Diagnostic & Statistical Manual of Mental Disorders, 4th Edition, Text Revision (DSM-IV-TR)** uses five **axes** to make a diagnostic summary:
• **Axis I**: Major Psychiatric Syndromes or Clinical Disorders
• **Axis II**: Personality Disorders and Mental Retardation
• **Axis III**: General Medical Conditions
• **Axis IV**: Psychosocial and Environmental Problems
• **Axis V**: Global Assessment of Functioning Score (0-100)

The DSM-IV-TR also uses Axis II to record prominent **personality traits** and **defense mechanisms**. For example, if a patient meets most of the criteria necessary for a paranoid personality disorder, this is recorded as "Paranoid Personality Features." If a personality disorder or strong features are not evident, but the patient uses a defense mechanism to a maladaptive level, this is recorded as "Frequent Use of Projection." Other official entries for coding on Axis II can be "No Diagnosis" or "Diagnosis Deferred." Two or more personality disorders can be diagnosed at the same time. Usually one is more pronounced and this is recorded as the main Axis II diagnosis, with prominent traits listed as "features" instead of a disorder. If two or more PDs are present to an equal extent, then they are all recorded. The residual personality diagnosis is called **personality disorder not otherwise specified (NOS)**. This is used when the patient does not meet sufficient criteria for a single personality disorder.

Personality & Culture

The DSM-IV-TR is prepared and published by the APA for use with culturally diverse populations. Personality disorder criteria in particular can be difficult to apply across cultural situations. Concepts of self, coping mechanisms, and modes of emotional expression vary considerably between cultures. However, the **World Health Organization (WHO)** emphasizes the similarity in psychiatric illnesses between nations and that diagnostic constructs are applicable regardless of culture. The increasing amount of information about genetic contributions in psychiatric disorders supports this view. Paris (1991) reported on the WHO multi-site investigation of personality disorder diagnoses on four continents. He found that the majority of diagnoses made would have been applicable in all centers.

Axis I & Axis II Disorders

Personality-disordered patients are more likely to develop Axis I disorders than the general population. Mood, anxiety, and substance-related disorders are common **comorbid conditions**. Major psychiatric disorders complicate the treatment of personality disorders and vice versa. Ascribing symptoms to a particular condition can be difficult because Axis I and II conditions often arise from similar vulnerabilities and processes. Age of onset, chronicity, and severity are not generally helpful in distinguishing personality disorders from major psychiatric conditions. A personality disorder, which may well be the priority for treatment, is often overlooked when an Axis I disorder co-exists. Assigning a separate axis for personality disorders (which started with the DSM-III), helped highlight the need to consider personality disorders and maladaptive traits. In general, a coexisting personality disorder has the following effects on major mental illnesses:

- Earlier age of onset
- Worsening of the course (including suicide attempts)
- Poorer and less predictable response to treatment
- Higher rate of recurrence/relapse of the illness
- Lowered compliance with treatment (for either condition)

Personality Change Due to a Medical Condition

Organic disorders are those resulting from medical illnesses, the effects of medications, or drugs of abuse. It is imperative to investigate the possibility that a personality change is being caused by organic factors. Psychiatric disorders with an organic etiology can be indistinguishable from those with purely psychological causes. In the DSM-IV-TR, this is called **personality change due to a medical condition**. This diagnosis is made when a personality disturbance is due to the direct physiological effects of a medical condition. When this is diagnosed, it is coded on Axis I as "Personality Change Due to. . .(Condition)." The medical condition is specified on Axis III. For example:

Axis I: Personality Change Due to Hypothyroidism
Axis III: Hypothyroidism

Personality Disorders as Milder Forms of Major Psychiatric Disorders

A major area of research in psychobiology involves conceptualizing personality disorders as being on a continuum with Axis I disorders, which is called the **dimensional model**. A useful analogy is that of someone being heterozygous for a single gene disease — often called **Mendelian diseases** — such as Huntington's disease or cystic fibrosis. Those who have a mixture of one affected and one non-affected gene may show an illness to a lesser extent, or not at all. If the degree of severity of the symptoms of Axis I conditions is lessened, there is an overlap with the core features of personality disorder clusters, which is as follows:

- *Schizophrenia/Psychotic Disorders* overlap with the Cluster A personality disorders — described as odd, eccentric, and socially detached.
- *Mood Disorders/Impulse-Control Disorders* overlap with Cluster B personality disorders and share the following traits: shifting emotions, externalizing emotions, and impulsivity.
- *Anxiety Disorders* overlap with Cluster C personality disorders and share: significant social avoidance, low tolerance for anxiety, and overly constrained behavior.

Ego Defenses

Another way of looking at PDs is to understand the use of ego defense mechanisms, also called ego defenses. People with PDs either use primitive ego defenses, or use more adaptive ones to such an extreme that they become maladaptive. Use of prominent ego defenses is also listed on Axis II.

What is Ego Psychology?

The unconscious mind uses a type of thinking called **primary process** which is not bound by logic, permits contradictions to coexist, contains no negatives, has no regard for time, and is highly symbolized. Primary process is seen in dreams, psychosis, and children's thinking. The preconscious and conscious mind use **secondary process** thinking, which is logical and deals with the demands of external reality. Secondary process is the goal-directed, day-to-day type of thinking used by adults. Freud developed his **structural theory** involving the **id**, **ego**, and **superego**. The **id** is completely unconscious and seeks gratification of instinctual (mainly sexual and aggressive) drives. The **superego** forms from an identification with the same-sex parent at the resolution of the **oedipal conflict**. It suppresses instinctual aims and serves as the "conscience." The **ego** is the mediator between the id and superego, and between the person and reality. The ego has both conscious and unconscious elements. The following are considered the conscious roles of the ego:

- Perception
- Affect
- Synthetic functions
- Reality Testing
- Thinking and Learning
- Control of instinctual drives

The fundamental concept in ego psychology is one of conflict between the **id**, **ego**, and **superego**. This conflict alerts the ego that a **defense mechanism** is required which is an unconscious role of the ego.

Principal Ego Defenses Operative in PDs

Antisocial   Acting Out, Controlling, Dissociation, Projective Identification

Avoidant   Displacement, Inhibition, Isolation, Projection

Borderline   Acting Out, Dissociation, Distortion, Projective Identification, Splitting

Dependent   Idealization, Inhibition, Projective Identification, Reaction Formation, Regression, Somatization

Histrionic   Denial, Dissociation, Regression, Repression, Sexualization

Narcissistic	Idealization/Devaluation, Identification, Projection
Obsessive-Compulsive	Displacement, Intellectualization, Isolation of Affect, Rationalization, Undoing
Paranoid	Denial, Projection, Projective Identification, Reaction Formation, Splitting
Schizoid	Devaluation, Idealization, Intellectualization, Introjection, Projection, Schizoid Fantasy
Schizotypal	Denial, Distortion, Idealization, Projection, Schizoid Fantasy

The illustration depicts the ego defense of **projection** (the best defense is a good offence).

Treatment of Personality Disorders

Psychotherapy, which is the major form of treatment for patients with personality disorders, can be defined as:

Treatment by communication for any form of mental illness, behavioral maladaptation, and/or other problem that is of an emotional nature, in which a trained person deliberately establishes a professional relationship with a patient for the purpose of:

• *Removing, modifying, or reducing existing symptoms*

• *Attenuating or reversing disturbed patterns of behavior*

• *Promoting positive personality growth and development*

Source: Campbell (1996)

Treatment of Personality Disorders

"ABCDEFGHIJKLM"'

• **A**ddiction
• **B**ehavioral
• **C**ognitive
• **D**rug (medications)
• **E**CT (electroconvulsive therapy)
• **F**amily Therapy
• **G**roup Therapy
• **H**ospitalization (partial, day or inpatient)
• **I**nsight-Oriented (psychoanalysis, psychotherapy)
• **J**ob (vocational rehabilitation)
• **K**nowledge (patient and family education)
• **L**eisure (art therapy, music therapy, crafts groups, etc.)
• **M**arital and relationship counseling

There are several places where interventions can be made in the scheme shown on page 15:

• Perception	Psychoactive Medication
• Thinking	Cognitive Therapy
• Feeling	Psychodynamic Psychotherapy
• Behaving	Behavior Therapy
• Social functioning	Group & Interpersonal Therapy
• Occupational abilities	Skills Training

relaxation
visualization

Understanding Mental Illness

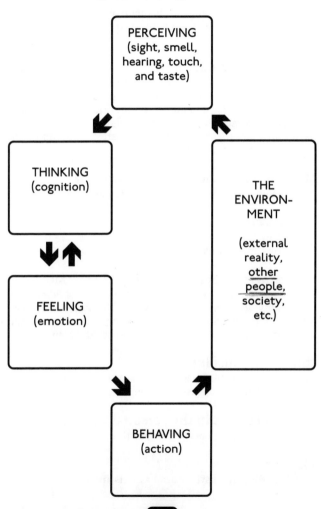

Organization of this Book

This book devotes a complete chapter to each of the DSM-IV-TR personality disorders. The chapters are organized into the following sections:

Title Page With Caricature

The artwork at the beginning of each chapter is included to appeal to two of your senses — vision, and your sense of humor. The author hopes that by adding a caricature to the presentation, readers will be able remember the material more readily by having an image to connect it with. No disrespect was intended for patients or their families.

Mnemonic for the Diagnostic Criteria

The mnemonics are based on DSM-IV-TR criteria.

Movie Examples

The names of the specific characters (not actors) are included in brackets after the name of the movie.

Portrayals of A Personality Type in the Movies

Movies are a great way to learn psychiatry — you may spot more personality-disordered characters with this description. The author is interested in receiving movie recommendations! You can submit your suggestions to: **rapid@psychler.com**

Interview Considerations

Diagnoses in psychiatry are all made clinically in interview situations. This section gives you some idea of what to expect.

Themes Present in the Personal History

This section supplements the diagnostic criteria.

Etiology

Both biological and psychosocial aspects are presented.

Epidemiology
Where known, the prevalence of each PD is given.

Differential Diagnosis
Primary psychiatric disorders (Axis I conditions), general medication conditions, and substance-related disorders must be considered before diagnosing a PD.

Mental Status Examination
The section supplements interview considerations to help further the recognition of PDs.

Psychodynamic Aspects
A brief understanding of the PD is given, which is based on psychoanalytic or psychodynamic theory.

Psychodynamic Therapy
Therapeutic interventions are outlined based on psychodynamic aspects.

Pharmacotherapy
While medications do not provide definitive therapy, certain symptoms can be targeted for pharmacologic treatment.

Group Therapy
Group therapy is a helpful and efficient method of treating PDs.

Cognitive Therapy
Time-limited, structured therapies are becoming increasingly effective and popular types of psychotherapy for PDs.

Course
A brief discussion of the overall course of the illness is given. This section obviously does not apply to the progress or changes possible for any particular person.

Chapter 2.
The Schizoid
Personality

The schizoid personality disorder (SzdPD) is characterized by social isolation (extending even to family members), a restricted range of emotional expression, and a lack of interest in almost all activities. Physical intimacy is not desired. Schizoid patients prefer solitary pursuits, often with a degree of intellectual abstraction — computers, mathematics, astronomy, electronics, etc. They come across as bland, distant people lacking social graces. Their restricted affect does not inspire others to engage them in conversation or pursue a relationship.

Mnemonic for Diagnostic Criteria — "SIR SAFE"

Solitary lifestyle
Indifferent to praise and criticism
Relationships are of little to no interest

Sexual experiences are not of interest
Activities preferred are almost always solitary
Friendships are few
Emotionally cold and detached

Movie Examples
- *Flesh and Bone* (Arlis Sweeney)
- *For A Few Dollars More* (Manco/The Man With No Name)
- *Léon/The Professional* (Léon)
- *Mad Max* (Max Rockatansky)

SzdPD in the Movies
Schizoid characters are socially detached, stolid, and prefer to fade into the woodwork rather than be noticed. Hence, they make for fairly uninteresting movie characters. Frequent portrayals involve loners, hermits, and outcasts. Perhaps the most common depiction is the hero of western movies. The stranger rides into town, reluctantly gets involved in some unfair situation, does his bit to further the common good, and then promptly leaves, declining the warm thanks of the townsfolk and the advances of an attractive woman. There is one feature

of SzdPD that is sometimes capitalized on in movies — their rich fantasy lives. While being externally bland, many schizoid individuals find considerable gratification in abstract activities such as role-playing games, at times with a sadomasochistic orientation.

Interview Considerations

Schizoid patients seem at best modestly cooperative when interviewed. Often responses are limited to a word or two, leaving the impression that the person would be indifferent towards significant or even catastrophic events. It is difficult to use a "strategy" to draw these people out. Often, general questions are used at the beginning of an interview to generate rapport. Schizoid patients' clipped responses may give the impression that they are upset, but this is an unlikely situation. Because they radiate little to no emotional warmth, it is difficult to use empathy to make a connection. Open-ended questions often do not evoke the desired response. Encouragement to provide more information, even on topics that interest these patients, rarely succeeds. If a history cannot be obtained using open-ended questions, a closed-ended, structured "laundry list" of questions may be necessary.

Schizoid Themes

- Prefers to do things alone
- Withdrawn and reclusive
- Lacks interests and hobbies
- No desire for relationships
- Deficient motivation
- Aloof, distant, and cold
- Constricted emotions

Etiology

Biological: SzdPD has a debatable link to schizophrenia. Some studies consider it a personality variant consistent with the **negative symptoms of schizophrenia**. Other studies suggest that the schizotypal personality disorder has a stronger association with, and a similar outcome to, schizophrenia. Temperamental factors include hyper-reactivity, a tendency towards being easily over-stimulated, anhedonia, and an aversion to others. Introversion is a highly heritable trait, with pupillary dilatation, elevated heart rate, and elevated urinary catecholamines accompanying this aversive behavior.

Psychosocial: A common family history involves cold, distant, inadequate, or even neglectful caregivers. Children raised in such a setting experience relationships as painful and unrewarding. However, the other extreme may also contribute to the etiology of this disorder. Parents who are over-involved and over-invested may foster an emotional withdrawal in their children. A common finding is that of a seductive mother who transgressed boundaries, and an impatient, critical father. **Bateson** coined the term **double bind** (the psychiatric equivalent of a *Catch-22*) to describe confusing and contradictory interactions. This no-win situation may facilitate retreat into a fantasy state.

Epidemiology

Estimates of prevalence range from 0.5 to 7%. By its nature SzdPD is difficult to record accurately. There may be a higher prevalence in males.

Differential Diagnosis

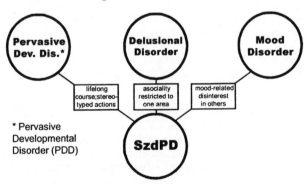

Mental Status Examination

- **Appearance:** None characteristic; usually inattentive to trends; clothes are functional, not fashionable; may appear to be socially inept
- **Behavior:** Edgy, anxious; fidgety; clumsy; stilted; ill at ease; few facial expressions; little animation
- **Cooperation:** Cooperative, but offer little information
- **Affect:** Restricted range, flat, withdrawn; may be dysphoric
- **Speech:** Goal directed but lacks detail; intonation rarely changes; monotonous; may be slow
- **Thought Content:** Little to no elaboration on any topic; one-word answers; seemingly unaffected by material usually laden with emotion; may be aware of having a lack of interest in people or significant events; may have ideas of reference (an event pertains to them specifically, such as a radio broadcast)
- **Thought Form:** No characteristic abnormality
- **Perception:** No characteristic abnormality
- **Insight & Judgment:** Intact; not bothered by lack of interest; tend to be pessimistic and underestimate their abilities
- **Suicide/Homicide:** Not likely to be a risk to others or themselves; isolation tends to minimize a disturbance in interpersonal functioning as a precipitant for seeking help

Psychodynamic Aspects

To schizoid patients, the world looms with the potential for consuming, engulfing, or absorbing them. The usual appetitive drives (sex, food, etc.) are not experienced as coming from within, but instead as coming from the external world. Emotional expression causes anxiety ranging from outright fear to deep ambivalence. When overwhelmed, these patients literally hide as a means of defense. It would be a mistake, however, to assume that no emotional experiences occur within these patients. Schizoid patients can be in touch with emotions on a level of genuineness not often seen. Difficulties may stem from a lack of validation of emotional and intuitive experiences, not their complete absence. Schizoid patients perceive what others ignore, and may feel out of place with those who are oblivious to what is so apparent to them. Social practices may appear so contrived that participation seems fraudulent. A detached and faintly contemptuous attitude helps to fend off a world perceived as over-controlling and over-intrusive.

Psychodynamic Therapy

Schizoid characters may be unfairly thought of as lower functioning across a spectrum of behaviors (social, career, interpersonal, etc.) due to the presumed connection to schizophrenia, and in particular, to the negative symptoms of that illness. It is important to keep in mind that this diagnosis can be applicable at any level of functioning — from a withdrawn, chronically hospitalized patient to a reclusive and highly creative artist.

It is common for schizoid patients to be drawn to intellectual pursuits often removed from direct contact with others — philosophy, theoretical sciences, mathematics, theological studies, computers, and creative arts. Overall level of functioning is not related exclusively to occupational functioning. The customary boundaries of time limits, the professional office setting, ethical restrictions against social and sexual relationships, and a clearly outlined therapeutic contract can all decrease fears of engulfment. Frequently, a crisis may precipitate the initial visit — an Axis I disorder (depression, anxiety), dysphoria over a loss, or the wish for a limited social life (schizoid individuals often long for unattainable sexual partners while ignoring available ones). Though they experience emotional pain, patients may not be able to clearly express themselves, and leave awkward pauses. It is important early on to create an atmosphere of patience, respect, and safety. By letting patients share *what* they want to, *in the way* they want to, and *at the speed* they want to, a trusting relationship has a chance to develop.

Imagination can be reframed as a talent, rather than being an immutable barrier. A key factor that promotes self-esteem is the encouragement of self-expression through creative activity.

Schizoid patients frequently need reassurance that they are not deviant or grotesque to others. Here, confirmation of their sensitivity and uniqueness can be valuable. This can be accomplished by communicating that their inner world is not only comprehensible, but that they have unique gifts, which can be aided by the use of artistic or literary examples. Patients can internalize the experience of being accepted without being engulfed or dominated. With an increase in self-esteem, patients can entertain the idea that their being misunderstood may well be due to the limitations of others, not solely because of personal deficiencies.

Pharmacotherapy

The rationale for the use of medication is based on the overlap of personality characteristics with the **negative symptoms of schizophrenia** and depression. Target symptoms can be:

- Apathy/decreased motivation
- Decreased libido
- Seclusiveness/social withdrawal
- Anhedonia
- Blunted affective responses

Newer antipsychotics improve **negative** or **deficit symptoms** to a greater degree than do traditional agents. Because there is also an overlap with symptoms of depression, antidepressant medications may provide some benefit. While any antidepressant may be efficacious, some of the **serotonin-specific reuptake inhibitors** (SSRIs) in particular may be helpful when anxiety is present.

Group Therapy

Some schizoid patients are suited to the group process. Meeting with a consistent group of people is an important step in beginning to value relationships and developing a social network. Social learning, such as the deciphering of facial expressions, gestures and verbal cues, is a common early therapeutic gain. At times, schizoid patients can be accused of passively drawing attention to themselves by remaining silent. Their detached manner can also be reminiscent of a co-therapist, and both these situations can draw ire from the more attention-seeking members of a group. If a therapist experiences countertransference difficulties with silence, he or she may covertly encourage group members to "gang up" on withdrawn patients. However, forcing patients to contribute too early to a group situation can be countertherapeutic because it repeats earlier interpersonal trauma.

Cognitive Therapy
Basic Cognitive Assumptions
- "I'm a social outcast."
- "Nothing excites me."
- "Relationships are just trouble."
- "Life is a lot easier without involving others."
Adapted from Beck, Freeman & Associates (1990)

Cognitive therapy with schizoid patients is a test of perseverance for the therapist. Because thoughts are linked to feelings, and since these patients express few feelings, it takes a considerable amount of time to generate something to examine. Also, the indifference expressed towards others removes a useful catalyst for change. Often these patients enter therapy because of anxiety or depression. While they are undergoing cognitive therapy for these conditions, interventions can be made toward correcting their isolated lifestyle:
- Paying more attention to positive emotional details
- Using limited self-disclosure to help develop rudimentary relationships
- **Social skills training** and **assertiveness training**

Course
SzdPD appears to be a stable condition. Little is known about patients' potential for developing psychotic illnesses over time.

Chapter 3.
The Paranoid
Personality

The paranoid personality disorder (PPD) is characterized by a generalized, unwarranted suspiciousness, and the tendency to misinterpret the actions of others as threatening or deliberately harmful. Other features of PPD are: a strong, disproportionate reaction to setbacks, hypersensitivity to criticism, and the aggressive pursuit of individual rights (when such rights are not being threatened).

Mnemonic for Diagnostic Criteria — "HEAD FUG"

Hidden meanings read into others' remarks and actions
Exploitation is automatically expected from others
Attacks on his or her character are perceived
Doubts the loyalty of others

HUGS FAR

Fidelity of partner is doubted
Unjustified suspicions about others
Grudges are held for lengthy periods of time

Suspects others of exploitation, deceipt + harm

Movie Examples
- *Falling Down* (William Foster)
- *Shine* (Peter Helfgott)
- *The Caine Mutiny* (Lt. Cmdr. Philip Francis Queeg)
- *FEAR (Reese with expoon)*

PPD in the Movies
Paranoid people are often portrayed in movies as individuals who are pitted against grim, faceless organizations such as greedy corporations or secret government agencies. Frequently, the main character has skills or knowledge that would be of use to "the bad guys" and he or she must convince skeptical friends that something sinister is going on. However, if someone is really being pursued or persecuted, then it isn't paranoia.

Another common portrayal of paranoid patients involves their litigious nature. They are intolerant of even minor or unintentional slights, and often play the role of the friendless, cranky person who brings frivolous legal action against others. A more positive depiction involves someone who keeps track of a seemingly minor piece of information (such as the license plate of a double-parked car) that turns out to be important in solving a major crime.

Interview Considerations

Paranoia of moderate (or greater) severity is usually not difficult to recognize. Hypervigilance, anger, hostility, and vindictiveness become obvious early in the interview. Considerable energy is expended trying to foil the efforts of those whom patients perceive as trying to shame or humiliate them. In most instances, these convictions are revealed readily, with a long list of justifications. Over time, patients become aware that others see them as paranoid and they can suppress their tirades, especially when there is an obvious gain in doing so (e.g. avoiding hospitalization).

With higher-functioning patients, paranoia can be much less obvious and detected only over time. For example, a request for assertiveness training or relaxation therapy may be veiled paranoia. The key question to keep in mind is *why* the request is being made. Further investigation might reveal a sense of being picked on, or not being able to relax because of constant vigilance.

Interviewing paranoid patients can be difficult because they expect to be exploited, taken advantage of, or even humiliated. Questions and intentions will be scrutinized for "hidden" meanings. Frequently, inquiries are made about how information will be used. Issues of confidentiality may be magnified. Regardless of how the interview is conducted, a lack of trust predominates. Paranoid thinking lacks flexibility, but highlighting obvious logical incongruities usually has no impact. Being genuine, open, and frank is more likely to be successful. An intervention that might be helpful involves pointing out how everything is twisted to fit their expectations.

Paranoid Themes

- Externalize blame for difficulties — see themselves as the continual target of abuse; constantly complain about poor treatment
- Have repeated difficulties dealing with authority figures; unable and unwilling to follow the lead of others
- Overestimate minor events — "Make mountains out of molehills"
- Search intensively to confirm suspicions to the exclusion of more reasonable conclusions — "Miss the forest for the trees"
- Cannot relax; have little to no sense of humor
- Projection of envy or even pathological jealousy onto others — "They're out to get me because they want what I have"
- Critical of those whom they see as weaker or needy
- Create their own environment based on subjective expectation, not objective attributes (called a **pseudocommunity**)

Etiology

Biological: Chess and Thomas found the following temperamental qualities were associated with paranoid disorders later in life: biological irregularity, non-adaptability, high intensity of reaction, negative mood, and a tendency to hyperactivity. Innate aggression or irritability may result in the angry and threatening qualities seen in this disorder.

First-degree relatives of those affected with schizophrenia have a higher incidence of PPD. This disorder is considered part of the **schizophrenic spectrum**. It is not uncommon for those who develop late-onset schizophrenia to have had PPD premorbidly. Paranoid traits have also been associated with developmental handicaps (e.g. impaired vision or hearing).

Psychosocial: Paranoid patients have often had repeated experiences of feeling overwhelmed and humiliated during childhood. Environmental factors often include: criticism, teasing, ridicule, arbitrary punishment, parents who cannot be pleased, and being used as a scapegoat. Children become vigilant for cues to impending sadistic treatment from caregivers, leading to their defensive attitude.

Children who grow up in environments filled with condemnation incorporate parental warnings about the outside world, even though they may find more kindness outside their homes. Children are often warned that outsiders have persecutory or exploitative goals. However, when someone from outside the family treats such a child decently, reality and feelings become incongruous. Fear and shame become instilled instead of a sense of being understood.

Children raised in such a milieu may also learn to believe that their feelings and complaints have a strong destructive power. Negative interactions with parents (e.g. being insulted) increase anger and frustration, and magnify the confusion about feelings and perceptions.

Epidemiology

The very nature of PPD makes it difficult to study and assess accurately. Estimates of prevalence range from 0.5% to 2.5%. No gender differences have consistently been reported.

Differential Diagnosis

Mental Status Examination

- **Appearance:** None characteristic; patients may be wary and have shifting eyes; in some cases physical abnormalities or sensory deficits may be present
- **Behavior:** Hypervigilant, anxious, tense
- **Cooperation:** Suspicious, guarded, challenging
- **Affect:** Anxious, hostile, humorless
- **Speech:** Fluent; goal directed; can be very articulate
- **Thought Content:** Patients will try to decipher your "true" intentions and can be quite confrontational when they believe they have been betrayed (such as their medical information being revealed to others); otherwise, they will generally speak about the plots and conspiracies of others; may have the belief that events (such as news events, radio broadcasts, etc.) pertain specifically to them (called **ideas of reference**)
- **Thought Form:** No characteristic abnormality
- **Perception:** Heightened awareness to all stimuli
- **Insight & Judgment:** Continually justify suspiciousness and hypervigilance
- **Suicide/Homicide:** More likely to be a risk to others than to themselves, may be self-injurious to preempt danger or catastrophic consequences that are seen as inevitable

Psychodynamic Aspects

At the core of this diagnosis is extremely low self-esteem. Paranoid personalities are outwardly demanding, superior, mistrustful, vigilant, lacking in sentimentality, and moralistic. Internally, they are timid, plagued with doubt, gullible, unable to grasp the big picture, and can be quite inconsiderate. They exude a stilted, grandiose manner in an attempt to compensate for their inner selves. They give special attention to those with a higher rank or more power as they desire strong allies, but are also fearful of being attacked.

Self-referential grandiosity is evident in that everything patients notice somehow directly relates to them. Self-esteem is enhanced by battling authority and people of importance.

Feelings of vindication and moral triumph provide a fleeting sense of safety and righteousness. They are litigious and live out the need to challenge a persecutory parent.

Paranoid patients are constantly warding off humiliation and transform any sense of their own culpability into a threat from the outside. They are fearful of shocking others with their depravity. For this reason, intimacy is avoided. They expect to be "found out" and are continuously trying to find the evil intent in others' behavior. To a paranoid person, showing weakness invites an attack. Because of past experiences, and the unacceptability of unconscious yearnings for closeness, intimacy is avoided. Love is feared as much as hate. Wishes for closeness are abhorred, denied, and projected.

Psychodynamic Therapy

The ultimate goal with paranoid patients is to create trust via a solid working alliance. When trust is truly achieved, the therapeutic process has been successful. The process of acknowledging weaknesses, making disclosures, and attempting an enduring relationship are important steps in treatment.

There is a strong tendency to try and talk patients out of their persecutory thoughts. Because people are not universally benevolent, it is difficult to persuade patients against being bothered by the "clues" they uncover. In fact, patients may perceive the attempt as a ploy to get their guard down, with the possible outcome of increasing their level of suspicion. It is more helpful to avoid confronting paranoid ideas. To do this, adopt a "let's agree to disagree" understanding. Paranoid patients are attuned to the emotions and attitudes of those around them. Their disorder involves a *misperception* of what happens, not missing the details. Challenging their beliefs is seen as an overt comment on their sanity, not on the fact that they have misinterpreted aspects of their environment.

If you are asked directly about your beliefs, try to use empathic statements that validate their feelings but offer alternative explanations. For example, "I can see why you are upset about people at work talking about you. Anyone would find that uncomfortable. However, could it be possible, just possible, that there is another explanation for what is happening?" This at least opens the door to a future re-examination by patients but gives them the option, in the short term, of feeling supported and taking or leaving what you've said.

The usual practices in psychotherapy are less likely to be successful with paranoid patients. Interpretations that attempt to probe the depth of their conflicts are not going to be graciously received. Consistency is another critical element in the therapeutic process. Regardless of the details of how therapy is carried out (missed sessions, telephone calls, vacations etc.), it is important to be consistent.

A maxim in psychotherapy is to "analyze resistance before content." In the interest of building an alliance, it may be better to provide straightforward answers to patients' questions. Giving answers, instead of trying to get at a deeper meaning, conveys an openness and genuineness lacking in their experiences with others.

Another technique is to search for precipitants when patients are upset. By avoiding confrontation and focusing on the cause, paranoid thinking can be altered. When patients do this outside of therapy, fear of malevolence from others gradually gives way to a focus on their own motives. Patients also learn by modeling. Patients can learn from their therapist's capacity to experience baser feelings and emotions without acting on them. One does not become bad or evil for simply having thoughts. Patients can come to enjoy feelings and fantasies and use therapy to discuss them. By making a distinction between thoughts and actions, they can learn that it is acceptable to have morbid fantasies.

Pharmacotherapy

Antipsychotic medications have been tried with limited success in treating PPD. When indicated, low doses of newer agents are used initially. In general, improvement occurs when the affect associated with the paranoid thoughts lessens, rather than seeing a clear decrease in persecutory thinking. Brief psychotic episodes, lasting from minutes to hours, can occur.

SSRIs are useful for decreasing obsessional features, feelings of anxiety, and mood symptoms. Reduction of anxiety in particular is necessary before other types of treatment can begin. Paranoid patients are generally known to be both wary and intolerant of side-effects, so a thorough explanation of potential reactions is required.

Cognitive Therapy

Cognitive strategies stress the use of action over words to help develop trust. The initial task is to increase self-efficacy through improving coping skills, or if these skills are adequate, enhancing patients' *sense* of self-efficacy. If they feel confident that they can handle the "attacks" of others, they will be less bothered by them. The next step involves modifying basic assumptions and interpersonal reactions. For example:

Basic Assumption: "The world is a rotten place. It's a dog-eat-dog world and if you aren't careful, you'll get chewed up and spit out."

Interpersonal Reaction: Sees others as threats and alienates them with poor treatment (e.g. unjustified accusations or unwarranted suspicion).

Result: Other people (understandably) react harshly, which tends to reinforce the rationale for the patient's negative basic assumptions.

The next focus is on testing their negative views by trusting others with small matters and evaluating the outcome. By doing so, patients become aware that the world has a spectrum of people in it ranging from malevolent to benevolent. Other interventions that can be used are:

- Teaching patients to attend to a wider range of social stimuli, not just the ones that they selectively notice
- Encouraging adjustments in appearance, grooming, mannerisms, tone of voice, and other factors that other people will notice immediately

Group Therapy

Paranoid patients generally do poorly in group therapy due to their active misinterpretation of others' motives. A group of patients would also have difficulty in understanding and dealing with the ego defense of **projective identification**. Factors that make group therapy more likely to succeed are:

- A well-timed introduction — no active confrontational crises occurring in the group when paranoid patients begin therapy
- Well-balanced composition of the group
- Ability of the therapist to act as an ally for the paranoid patient

The ability of the group to provide paranoid patients with a consensus about unwarranted suspicions can be a powerful intervention.

Course

Comparatively little research has been conducted on PPD because it has a tradition of responding poorly to treatment. Patients readily find evidence from their surroundings and interactions with others to reaffirm their suspiciousness. Patients tend to have enduring problems at work and in relationships. Little is known about the longitudinal course of this disorder.

Chapter 4.
The Schizotypal Personality

The word *schizotypal* is a contraction of *schizophrenic genotype*. schizotypal personality disorder (SztPD) is characterized by deficits in interpersonal relationships and distortions in cognition and perception. Patients also exhibit peculiar behavior, exaggerated social anxiety, and idiosyncratic speech. SztPD shares an overlap with the **positive symptoms of schizophrenia** while the schizoid personality disorder overlaps more with the **negative symptoms**.

Mnemonic for Diagnostic Criteria — "UFO AIDER"

Unusual perceptions
Friendless except for family members
Odd beliefs, thinking and speech

Affect is inappropriate or constricted
Ideas of reference
Doubts others — suspicious and paranoid
Eccentric appearance and behavior
Reluctant in social situations

Movie Examples
- *Ghost* (Oda May Brown)
- *Grumpy Old Men* (Ariel Truax)
- *Hello Again* (Zelda)

SztPD in the Movies
Schizotypal characters are tailor made for roles such as fortune tellers, clairvoyants, mystics, psychics, mediums, mind readers, and guides to other worlds. The presumptive ability of these characters to predict the future or to make revelations about others enhances plot development. The visions, predictions, and warnings offered by schizotypal characters often turn into self-fulfilling prophecies. In some movies, they are connected to supernatural elements that magically cause or fix problems.

Interview Considerations

Schizotypal patients often seem unusual in interviews. Empathy and nonjudgmental acceptance of (but not agreement with) their irrational perceptions is necessary in order to establish rapport. Once this is achieved, persistent inquisitiveness on the interviewer's part will help uncover the sanctuary of the patient's unusual ideas. Often schizotypal patients reveal insights, eccentricities, and connections that make them sound like they come from another planet.

It is not usually difficult to maintain the interview once these patients feel accepted. Use facilitating techniques such as open-ended questions and ask for specific information and examples to illustrate answers. As long as patients feel you are interested and can appreciate their experiences, they will be cooperative.

In a well-conducted interview, schizotypal patients may sense a connection, and ask if you share the same views. In this situation, it is important to preserve the tone you have set. Do not dismiss their views or prematurely confront them with reality. As in other difficult situations, "agree to disagree" on the idea/point/issue in order to preserve rapport.

Schizotypal Themes

- Clairvoyance
- Suspiciousness
- Emotional reasoning
- Reduced productivity
- Premonitions
- Existential concerns
- Magical thinking
- Flat, emotionless affective style

Etiology

Biological: The schizotypal personality disorder has a strong genetic link to schizophrenia. Adoption and family studies have consistently found an increased prevalence of **schizophrenic spectrum** disorders in the relatives of patients with SztPD. Similarly, there is an increased prevalence of SztPD in the relatives of patients with schizophrenia. Epidemiologic studies have shown the prevalence of SztPD to be three times that of schizophrenia in the general population. It may be that the SztPD is a milder and more common expression of the schizophrenic genetic diathesis. Biological and physiological findings in schizophrenia may also be abnormal in patients with SztPD:

- **Smooth pursuit eye movement** (SPEM) abnormalities — when following a moving object, rapid eye movements (**saccades**) occur instead of smooth, conjugate tracking.
- Elevated levels of **homovanillic acid** (HVA) in the cerebrospinal fluid and plasma may be associated with positive symptoms.
- An abnormally high **ventricle-brain ratio** (VBR) is seen on CT scans.

Psychosocial: The concordance rate for schizophrenia in monozygotic twins approaches fifty percent. Put another way, if one twin develops schizophrenia, the other has only a fifty percent chance of doing so. This emphasizes the role of psychosocial factors in the development of psychiatric disorders. Due to the relatively recent description of SztPD as a separate disorder, there are few theories about what may constitute a definite psychosocial contributor.

A number of psychosocial theories have been advanced regarding schizophrenia and may be operative in the pathogenesis of SztPD:

- **Social Causation** — this theory postulates that being a member of lower socioeconomic classes is significant in causing mental illness

- **Double Bind** — conflicting messages cause patients to withdraw into a regressed state to avoid unsolvable problems

- **Schisms and Skews** — these abnormal patterns of interaction within families leads to an unhealthy alignment of a parent with a child, or to an abnormally dominant caretaker

- **Expressed Emotion** (EE) — defined as family members showing hostility, criticism or becoming over-involved with patients; EE is an important educational point to stress with the families of affected individuals; reducing EE has therapeutic and prognostic implications

Given the genetic correlation with schizophrenia, and difficulties with cognitive processing, it can be hypothesized that such stimulus barriers could create difficulties at all stages of development. In the **vulnerability-stress model**, a person is genetically "loaded" (vulnerability or diathesis), and then a stressor causes the emergence of the disorder. The actual stress can take many forms:

- Parents who are too indulgent, neglectful, or authoritarian
- The threatened or actual break-up of a relationship
- Intrusion into a usually secretive, isolated lifestyle
- The stresses of leaving home and/or academic hardship

Epidemiology

The prevalence is estimated to be 3% of the population with no consistently reported gender difference. Women may display positive symptoms more frequently than men.

Differential Diagnosis

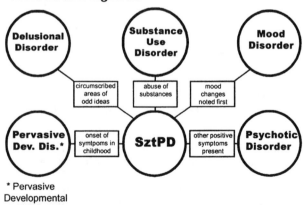

* Pervasive Developmental Disorder (PDD)

Mental Status Examination

- **Appearance:** Often peculiar; may have amulets, charms, odd jewelry; dress doesn't reflect social convention or current styles; accessories/colors may have special meaning
- **Behavior:** May be anxious towards a skeptical interviewer; behavioral oddities may include unusual facial expressions
- **Cooperation:** Cooperative in a receptive atmosphere
- **Affect:** Ranges from restricted/flat to animated
- **Speech:** Unusual or idiosyncratic meaning to some words; context can be odd; may use neologisms
- **Thought Content:** Paranoid ideas; suspiciousness; magical thinking; telepathy; premonitions; "sixth sense"; out of body experiences; bizarre coincidences; extra sensory perception
- **Thought Form:** No characteristic abnormality; may be tangential, circumstantial, vague or over-elaborate
- **Perception:** May have unusual perceptual experiences
- **Insight & Judgment:** Partial; may be aware others consider them odd; judgment is based heavily on their perception of reality (which is not verifiable by others)
- **Suicide/Homicide:** Need to consider this in conjunction with an Axis I disorder; not generally a risk to others or themselves; risk increases with the presence of a formal thought disorder or marked paranoia

Psychodynamic Aspects

The psychodynamic theories regarding schizophrenia and SztPD are similar and can be considered as varying mainly in degree of severity. Freud hypothesized that schizophrenic patients are fixated at an early stage of development. The resulting defects in ego structure facilitate psychotic regression in response to conflict or frustration. Additionally, Freud thought that schizophrenic patients reinvest psychic energy back into themselves instead of towards people around them. This contributes to the development of an autistic world with subjective thinking, introversion, and personal use of language, which are features also seen in SztPD. Some of the psychoanalytic concepts that pertain to the psychological factors in the etiology of schizophrenia are relevant to understanding the development of the SztPD:

- **Object constancy** is not achieved. This is defined as the ability to develop evocative memory and create a stable intrapsychic image of a caregiver. Without this, the person faces difficulty in progressing beyond the oral stage of development, typified by complete dependence on a caregiver. A defect in developing a separate identity predisposes a patient to a personality structure that is vulnerable to disintegration under stress. Due to the fixation of development at this early stage, primitive ego defenses are used.
- The conflict in psychosis is between the ego and the external world where reality is reconstructed via hallucinations, delusions, etc.
- Psychotic thought processes have a symbolic meaning for the patient. Schizotypal patients may be overwhelmed by stress and the demands placed on them. In response to this, they create an alternate reality that is more manageable and comprehensible. Perceptual abnormalities and delusions often represent inner wishes or fears. **Magical thinking** and ideas of influence represent wishes for child-like omnipotence over uncontrollable, unbearable, or unpleasant events.

An infant having temperamental difficulties with attachment may perceive his or her mother as rejecting, and then withdraw from her. However, the infant's needs grow until they seem insatiable. At this point, the infant may fear that greed will devour his or her mother, leading to subsequent abandonment. As adults, schizoid and schizotypal patients are affected by highly conflicting feelings — on the one hand fearing that their neediness will drive others away, but also fearing that others will devour them if they get too close (projected greed).

Psychodynamic Therapy

For all psychiatric conditions, a higher level of functioning prior to entering therapy generally predicts a better outcome. Diagnosis is not the only factor to consider in developing a treatment plan. A comprehensive assessment of a patient's strengths, coping skills, intelligence, and ability to form attachments is essential in guiding psychotherapy of any type.

In general, Cluster A patients are vulnerable to decompensation under stressful conditions. Along the continuum of techniques, a supportive focus is recommended over an exploratory or confrontational one. Typically, a "here and now" directive approach is useful.

The most frequent complication arises when patients seek to test their perceptions, or ask for reassurance about them. It may be more beneficial to address the feelings expressed (fear, sadness, etc.) with these unusual ideas and experiences than it is to be the arbiter of reality. Internalization of a non-judgmental relationship with a respectful, interested therapist is much more helpful for schizotypal patients than are interpretations regarding their use of psychic hotlines or other forays into alternative pursuits.

As in any therapy, an alteration in interpersonal style will frequently be met with resistance. In schizotypal patients, this is likely to take the form of silence because their fundamental difficulty is that of relating to other people (DSM-IV-TR criteria eight and nine). Just as with the expression of unusual perceptions and ideas, silence should be non-judgmentally accepted. Silence in this situation is a defensive retreat on the patient's part. As therapy proceeds, the therapist may need to serve as an auxiliary ego for the patient. Schizotypal patients have a tendency to misinterpret reality and focus on symbolic meanings, rather than on the intended or most obvious ones.

Pharmacotherapy

Intuitively, it seems that antipsychotic medication would be useful in SztPD. Neuroleptics are the mainstay of treatment for schizophrenia and work well for reducing positive symptoms, which are mainly those manifested in SztPD. Studies have looked at the use of antipsychotic and antidepressant medication, specifically the SSRIs. Overall the results revealed:

- Reductions in impulsivity and aggression with SSRIs
- Psychotic symptoms showed the best response to medication, especially cognitive/perceptual disturbances

Cognitive Therapy

Basic Cognitive Distortions:

- Mistrust, suspiciousness or frank paranoid ideation
- Ideas of reference — "There are special messages for me"
- Magical thinking — "I can make something happen by wishing for it"
- Illusory percepts — "Important historical figures visit me on a daily basis"

Adapted from Beck, Freeman & Associates (1990)

The automatic thoughts in SztPD often reveal the distortions of **emotional reasoning** and **personalization**. In emotional reasoning, the person experiences a distressing emotion and automatically forecasts a negative event. Personalization is similar to an idea of influence in that a person falsely believes he or she is responsible for an external situation.

After a working alliance has been established, cognitive strategies focus on increasing social appropriateness. This helps improve day-to-day functioning in the areas of hygiene, social skills, and personal management. These skills are reinforced through modeling, role-playing, structured sessions, and setting short-term goals that are frequently reviewed. The next step involves the critical aspect of teaching patients to look for objective evidence in the environment on which to evaluate their automatic assumptions. Along with this, patients are asked to consider the consequences of relying solely on their emotional responses. It is unlikely that these patients will ever completely eradicate their bizarre notions, but they can gain some emotional relief by recognizing inaccuracies.

Group Therapy

Group therapy can be of considerable benefit to schizotypal patients, particularly in the area of increasing their socialization skills. The group functions as an extended family providing corrective emotional experiences that increase schizotypal patients' comfort with others. Difficulties can arise with patients who are too bizarre, or too different from other members. Prolonged silences and lack of contribution may cause the group to ignore or ridicule schizotypal patients.

Course

The overlap of genetic, biological, and phenomenological findings with schizophrenia gives SztPD a more pessimistic outcome. At long-term follow-up, ten-to-twenty percent of patients go on to develop schizophrenia. The remainder appear to have a stable course. Three characteristics of this personality disorder have been positively correlated with later onset of schizophrenia: magical thinking, paranoid ideation, and social isolation.

Chapter 5.
The Histrionic
Personality

The word histrionic is derived from hysteria, a term originally used to describe phobias, dissociative and amnestic phenomena, as well as **somatoform disorders** (such as **conversion disorder** and **hypochondriasis**). Histrionic personality disorder (HPD) is characterized by excessive emotional expression and attention-seeking behavior.

Mnemonic for Diagnostic Criteria — "I CRAVE SIN"

Inappropriate behavior — seductive or provocative

Center of attention
Relationships are seen as closer than they really are
Appearance is most important
Vulnerable to the suggestions of others
Emotional expression is exaggerated

Shifting, **S**hallow emotions
Impressionistic manner of speaking which lacks detail
Novel situations are sought

Movie Examples
- *A Streetcar Named Desire* (Blanche DuBois)
- *Blue Sky* (Carly Marshall)
- *Born Yesterday* (Emma "Billy" Dawn)
- *Gone with the Wind* (Scarlett O'Hara)

HPD in the Movies
Histrionic characters are often cast in romantic roles and comedies. Their capricious style and vanity are qualities around which the plot can be built. They are good at attracting other characters and are naturals for "center of attention" situations. A classic pairing is that of a histrionic female with a male who has an obsessive-compulsive personality. Here, her unpredictability contrasts with his emotional constriction and pedantic nature. A variation on this theme sets the flair and *joie*

de vivre of a histrionic character against the rigid, oppressive rules of society.

Interview Considerations

Histrionic patients give dramatic and exaggerated interviews. Histories are often erratic with inconsistencies becoming obvious as more information is obtained. Open-ended questions usually lead to long, animated answers peppered with gestures, affectations, and segues. Despite the abundance of "talk" there is a paucity of detail. Answers are frequently vague and evasive, dealing with only superficial elements. Additionally, the outpouring of emotion lacks substance, with discrepancies readily observed between reported symptoms and genuine emotional investment. **La belle indifférence** refers to an obvious emotional detachment from symptoms. This is also seen in other conditions such as conversion disorder and strokes.

It is not usually difficult to initiate an interview with histrionic patients. In any setting, time is given at the outset for patients to "tell their story." They revel in this opportunity and respond to the attention of an interested listener. As the interview proceeds, there is a lot of "weather" but a lack of "news." Redirection does not usually affect the interview, as new topics are pursued with the same vigor.

Maintaining the structure of the interview requires redirecting answers back to the presenting complaint or another central focus. The major challenge is in obtaining complete and accurate information. Polite persistence, curbing answers, closed-ended questions, and asking for concrete examples will help complete the history.

Histrionic Themes

- Emotional instability
- Vanity
- Suggestibility
- Exhibitionism
- Sexual provocation
- Overly reliant on others

Etiology

Biological: There is an increased prevalence of HPD in the families of affected individuals. HPD and somatization disorder share an historical association. Some studies have found a genetic link between the two disorders as well as associations between HPD, ASPD, and substance-related disorders. Certain temperamental factors may predispose individuals to a histrionic personality style: intensity, hypersensitivity, extroversion, and reward dependence. There is a strong "orality" or appetitive desire within histrionic individuals. They crave love, attention and gratification, but can become overwhelmed by too much stimulation.

Histrionic people tend to give overly impressionistic answers to questions. In the left brain-right brain scheme, Histrionic people are considered to be right-brain dominant. Instead of answering questions, they give vivid impressions, whereas obsessive-compulsive personalities would be left-brain dominant.

Psychosocial: The family dynamics of HPD patients often reveal a power distribution that favored males (or was perceived as being so). A common feature is a father who was both intimidating and seductive. Narcissistic qualities such as criticism, angry outbursts, and selfishness transmit the message that males must be approached with caution. Some patients have fathers who turned to them for gratification not available in the marriage. The father who turned to open collusion, overt sexuality or even incest, creates the **approach-avoidance conflict** prominently seen in this disorder. Histrionic patients are fixated in a range between **oral** and **oedipal stages**. Neglectful parents may unconsciously or unwittingly encourage their children to become dramatic in order to get attention.

The **Oedipal complex** (**Electra complex** in females) is usually resolved by repression of impulses towards the opposite-sex parent, and identification with the same-sex parent. This resolution is not satisfactorily achieved in HPD because the patient:

- Rejects identification with her (devalued) mother
- Represses her sexuality to remain "Daddy's little girl"
- Learns she cannot possess her father and feels rejected

Epidemiology

The prevalence is estimated to be 3% of the population. There is a gender difference with women being diagnosed more frequently than men. Some studies have found an equal prevalence among men and women with rates as high as 15% in some psychiatric populations. Sociocultural factors are a key consideration in making this diagnosis (e.g. the cultural milieu in the movie *Gone with the Wind*).

Differential Diagnosis

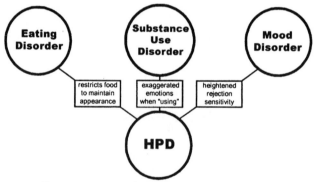

Mental Status Examination

- **Appearance:** Often very fashionable; pay particular attention to grooming, accessories, designer clothing, coloring hair
- **Behavior:** Vivid expressions; frequent, dramatic gestures
- **Cooperation:** Notably cooperative
- **Affect:** Wide range of affect expressed; can change quickly
- **Speech:** Animated, modulated voice
- **Thought Content:** Superficial descriptions; use colorful adjectives; global impressions lack detail; use hyperbole

- **Thought Form:** No characteristic abnormality; may be tangential, circumstantial, vague, or overelaborate
- **Perception:** No characteristic abnormality
- **Insight & Judgment:** Partial; often unaware of flirtatious manner; can place themselves in danger with their provocative speech and mannerisms
- **Suicide/Homicide:** Need to consider in conjunction with any Axis I disorder; can overreact to losses or abandonment

Psychodynamic Aspects

Histrionic individuals have unresolved oral and oedipal elements. This fixation is characterized by immaturity. Histrionic patients are like caricatures of femininity by appearing shallow, vain, dependent, and dramatic. Their internal existence is that of a helpless, fearful child trying to navigate in a world dominated by powerful figures. They fear intrusion (retaliation from mother) and rejection (losing father).

The central psychodynamic feature in histrionic patients is anxiety. The classical explanation is that ego defenses are recruited in response to **signal anxiety**, an unconscious process where the ego is mobilized against internal or external threats. In other personalities, sexual energy is expressed or sublimated, but histrionic patients have **repressed** their sexuality during development. However, repression is soon overwhelmed because this defense cannot adequately deal with normal impulses that are continually seek expression.

The DSM-IV-TR diagnostic criteria emphasize the behavioral aspects of HPD which achieve three goals for these patients:
- Security and sanctuary from an environment perceived as hostile
- Increasing self-esteem
- Provoking frightening situations in an attempt to master them

Histrionic patients see male figures as strong and exciting, but also dangerous. Because of their idealization of father figures, they are attracted to men they see as powerful, though this alliance remains steeped in conflict. Patients seek the protection that such men offer, while fearing abuse of this power, and may unconsciously hate men for it. Sexuality is used in a defensive manner instead of as a true expression of libido. Thus, patients can appear to be highly seductive, but are largely unaware of the sexual nature of their invitations, and are often surprised when their actions are interpreted as flirtatious. Should they proceed with the encounter, it may well be to reduce a perceived threat and the guilt which emerges after being confronted with accusations of seductive behavior. These factors drastically reduce the possibility of histrionic patients actually enjoying sexual experiences.

Histrionic patients, seeing their only strength as sexual attractiveness, become highly invested in appearance and have difficulties with aging. These patients also increase security and self-esteem by initiating frightening situations which they attempt to master. The term **counterphobic attitude** is used to describe behavior in which feared situations are sought out. **Acting out** is the process of living out an unconscious wish or impulse in order to avoid becoming aware of the idea or the emotion that accompanies it. Much like patients who take up activities such as parachuting after a heart attack, histrionic patients tend to act out their conflicts in counterphobic ways, often related to their preoccupation with the fantasied power and the dangerousness of the opposite sex. Examples include:
- Seductive behavior when sex is frequently not enjoyed
- Flirtatiousness which covers a sense of bodily shame
- Craving and attracting attention while feeling inferior to others

Because of early experiences, patients do not expect to be taken seriously or to receive respectful attention. As adults, they yearn for acceptance, but relate to others in ambiguous ways. Feelings are conveyed in a way that allows retraction in case patients are ignored by the more "powerful" people present. Coquettish mannerisms and flowery adjectives facilitate a retreat in such instances. Another view holds that the combination of intensity, shallowness, and impressionistic style defends against an awareness of stronger emotions.

The situation for histrionic males is similar to females. They also experience maternal deprivation and look to their fathers for nurturance. When this is not provided, some men develop an effeminate identity influenced by their mothers. Others model cultural stereotypes of hyper-masculinity.

Psychodynamic Therapy

Psychoanalysis was developed by Freud for the treatment of patients with hysteria/histrionic personality qualities. Psychodynamically-oriented psychotherapies remain a preferred treatment for HPD. Histrionic patients who function in a moderate or better range can thrive in psychotherapy. To a significant degree, they "make themselves well" without extensive guidance.

It is important to establish a therapeutic contract or working alliance as soon as possible. The parameters and goals of psychotherapy should be clearly explained and conveyed in an open, professional manner. Some patients have the expectation that therapists "know all about them" or "know them better than they know themselves." This perception needs to be corrected at the outset of therapy. Patients should be encouraged to be as open as possible about their feelings, regardless of the degree of embarrassment involved. Exploring reactions and resistance avoids making therapy an experience of submitting to yet another authority figure.

One of the first therapeutic interventions with histrionic patients is to obtain a detailed account of their present functioning and history. Redirection and persistence will be required to get past the "I don't know" and "I told you everything already" replies. By encouraging patients to be more reflective and attend to internal and external experiences in greater detail, repression is lessened. The increased amount of emotional information allows an examination of both ideas and feelings and, most importantly, the connection between the two.

Awareness of this association, with the ability to discuss thoughts and feelings in detail, increases the interest in, and tolerance for, deeper experiences. Histrionic patients express considerable interest in finding out about their therapists' private lives. This form of resistance becomes apparent at times of stress, either in or out of the therapeutic relationship. This defensive maneuver camouflages difficulties in accessing their own feelings. Regardless of the tenacity of such attempts, self-disclosure is ill-advised. While questions of a general nature can be answered, much can be gained by not gratifying the attempts at sexualizing the therapy. Psychotherapy helps patients develop autonomy when their desires are not exploited by the therapist (who represents a powerful figure). Exposure to someone who keeps the patient's best interests in mind is another benefit of psychotherapy.

As with all personality disorders, HPD occurs in a range of severity from the healthier "oedipal" to the less functional "oral" histrionics. Patients who function at lower psychological levels require a more active and educational approach. Such patients may particularly benefit from construction of a detailed history focusing on their maladaptive responses to anxiety. For example, pointing out that a wish to flee from therapy is part of the same process interfering with their relationships and jobs, helps patients gain some perspective and maintain the therapeutic relationship.

Lower-functioning patients are more prone to experience physical symptoms with emotional difficulties. Still, these symptoms have a psychodynamic relevance and an awareness of this is helpful in dealing with them. Conversion symptoms achieve the **primary gain** of anxiety reduction by resolving the conflict between having wishes and their prohibition. **Secondary gain** is a real-world advantage from others (attention from others, relief from duties, etc.). **Tertiary gain** refers to the benefit that others receive from the patient's secondary gain (e.g. financial support).

Group Therapy

Histrionic patients can present in assessments as charming, outgoing, and expressive. They are often chosen readily and can serve as valuable members in group therapy. Their energy activates passive members, and their seductiveness can stir transference reactions that help fuel group interaction.

However, there are drawbacks to having histrionic members in a group. Craving attention, they shift allegiances frequently and may escalate their dramatic ways if overshadowed by others. Flirtatious behavior may well attract more than one group member, creating a rivalry in addition to the one already existing between patients and the therapist.

Histrionic patients can also be seen as **help-rejecting complainers**. These individuals play the role of victim and induce caregiving behavior in others (advice giving, offering favors, etc.). When this is done, the patient devalues the effort and resumes complaining, which is a difficult situation to deal with in a group setting. Histrionic patients can benefit from group therapy when they understand that their loquaciousness and endless dissatisfaction serve to isolate them from others and perpetuate their unhappiness.

Cognitive Therapy
Basic Cognitive Distortions:
- "I am incapable of looking after myself. I can't do it on my own."
- "I need to have a powerful man's interest at all times."
- "If I'm not fun and exciting, no one will want me around."
Adapted from Beck, Freeman & Associates (1990)

The central cognition in HPD is, "I am inadequate and unable to manage by myself." This is not unique to HPD — it is also seen in depression and dependent personality disorder. Unlike patients with these two disorders, histrionic patients actively find others who will accept them and attend to their needs. This perpetuates a cycle in HPD. Patients feel they are inadequate, use emotional reasoning ("if I feel this way, I must be this way"), and then set out to find someone to take care of them, reinforcing their initial sense of inadequacy.

Histrionic patients are so focused on external approval and acceptance that they have little consideration left for their own internal existence. While capable of introspection, they do not naturally attend to details. Frequently, patients are not able to identify what they need, and avoid self-knowledge because it feels foreign. The cognitive-behavioral treatment of HPD is less well established than in other personality disorders. This type of therapy requires patience in examining thoughts and testing alternatives, which is contrary to the histrionic style. However, histrionic patients can benefit from the following interventions:

- Developing a more systematic, problem-focused style of thinking by setting a reasonable agenda and attending to one item at a time
- Considering the long-term costs of impulsivity; looking for alternatives such as pro/con tables for important decisions
- Assertiveness training, which may take time to work because patients fear rejection when they ask for what they want
- Role-playing with an element of rejection so patients learn ways to reduce their sense of embarrassment

It is important to reassure patients that their "basic character" will not be altered in cognitive therapy. On a practical level, patients can be encouraged to seek employment that satisfies their need for visibility: acting, dancing, politics, teaching, the arts, etc. Histrionic patients can be quite creative when integrating their emotions with their work.

Pharmacotherapy

With the wide fluctuation in mood and affect seen in this disorder, there may be a role for mood stabilizers when such episodes are sustained for at least a period of several days. Rejection sensitivity, irritability, and anxiety symptoms may respond well to antidepressants, particularly SSRIs and **monoamine oxidase inhibitors (MAOIs)**. From time to time, judicious use of sedative-hypnotics and anxiolytics may be needed to help patients through crises. Generally, medications play less of a role in the treatment of HPD than they do in other personality disorders.

Course

Little is known definitively about long-term outcome. As with other Cluster B disorders, it takes considerable energy to maintain this personality configuration. Patients may "burn out" and show fewer symptoms with time. Because HPD is among the Axis II disorders most amenable to therapeutic intervention, the outcome can be viewed optimistically.

Chapter 6.
The Antisocial
Personality

The antisocial personality disorder (ASPD) is characterized by guiltless, exploitative and irresponsible behavior with the hallmark being conscious deceit of others. ASPDs have a lifelong pattern (defined as being present prior to age fifteen years) of disregard for the rights of others. This disorder has also been called the **psychopathic** and **sociopathic** personality disorder. **Psychopathy** is defined as "a cluster of both personality traits and socially deviant behaviors." Criminal activity itself does not necessarily imply the presence of ASPD. Sociopathic patients are rarely distressed by their actions, and come to attention for other reasons. The most common reasons for psychiatric contact involve: detoxification, prescriptions for drugs with a street value, a note for missing work, a forensic assessment to relieve them of criminal responsibility, and avoiding military service or other work they consider undesirable (essentially areas of **secondary gain**).

Mnemonic for Diagnostic Criteria — "CALLOUS MAN"

Conduct disorder before age 15 years; current age at least 18 years
Antisocial activities; commits acts that are grounds for **A**rrest
Lies frequently
Lacunae — lacks a superego
Obligations are not honored (financial, occupational, etc.)
Unstable — can't plan ahead
Safety of self and others is ignored

Money — spouse and children are not supported
Aggressive, **A**ssaultive
Not occurring during schizophrenia or mania

Movie Examples

- *Bad Influence* (Alex)
- *Casino* (Nicky Santoro)
- *Man Bites Dog* (Benoît)
- *The Usual Suspects* (Roger "Verbal" Kint)

ASPD in the Movies

Popular media teems with antisocial characters. They fulfill the requirements of the "media id" — sex and violence — and are intriguing characters in dramas. Sociopaths are fascinating because they commit acts that strike at the core of moral society: murder, sexual assault, kidnapping, extortion, torture, etc. They carry out common fantasies of such behavior, satisfying many audience members' voyeuristic interests, and enhancing the action component of the film.

Interview Considerations

Antisocial patients can be easy or quite difficult to interview. They have what Kernberg has termed a **malignant grandiosity** — a *deliberate* attempt to use others as opposed to the more unconscious kind of manipulation seen in other personality disorders. Antisocial characters openly brag about con jobs, conquests, and scams to impress others. They will shamelessly try to put one over on you in the midst of telling you how successful they've been in deceiving others.

As long as there is an interest in hearing about these exploits, rapport is easily established. This can be subtly or even overtly encouraged, and needs to be developed before looking at more sensitive areas. For example, statements such as the ones below will have ASPDs eagerly waiting to tell you more.
- "You really seem to have a way with people."
- "You're a pretty smart guy."
- "You must have a lot of respect out on the street."

Once they realize that condemnation is not forthcoming, it is not difficult to maintain a positive atmosphere. It is important to remain morally neutral, and not do anything that might be misconstrued as approval for the antisocial acts mentioned. To ASPDs, this will seem like collusion. Difficulties begin when patients' manipulations are resisted, or their requests are refused. They can then become hostile, critical, derogatory, intimidating, and even violent.

If rapport is lost or difficult to initiate, it can be obtained by appealing to patients' sense of grandiosity. They strive to be the center of attention and may respond to an air of indifference from interviewers. By demonstrating that a particular interview is not one's only priority, and being vague about rescheduling, cooperation can be obtained. Also, if someone of "lesser" clinical rank is suggested as an alternative interviewer, patients may not bear the insult to their self-importance. ASPDs seek immediate gratification, and seize opportunities when they present themselves. Like patients with other personality disorders, ASPDs can be found at higher levels of functioning. Antisocial patients can be quite sophisticated, and may be able to deceive others with rehearsed lines and convincing explanations for their "dilemmas." This will be especially evident with remorse. Most will relate feeling bad about something, but this has more to do with being caught than genuine regret.

ASPDs tend to minimize their involvement or the outcome of their actions. Words are twisted to achieve this effect (for example "skirmish" or "spat" instead of fight). Language is used to manipulate others, which is an important clue in interviews.

Antisocial Themes
- Glibness, shallow emotion
- Requires constant stimulation
- Parole/probation violations
- Abuse of substances
- Grandiosity
- Poor impulse control
- Avoids responsibility
- Behavioral problems

Etiology
Biological: The antisocial personality disorder provides some of the strongest evidence for the heritability of personality disorders. Chess and Thomas found that as children, antisocial patients were innately aggressive with higher activity and reactivity levels and lowered consolability. This may indicate an inborn tendency toward aggression and a higher-than-average need for excitement.

Twin studies also indicate that a genetic factor is operative. Studies have shown a higher-than-societal average incidence of ASPD in the adopted-away children of antisocial biological parents (these studies included an evaluation for the presence of ASPD in adoptive parents). If such a genetic component exists, physical aberrations (particularly neurological) may serve as a marker. The following have been reported:

- Lower-than-average reactivity of the autonomic nervous system (also reported is an inability to learn from experience)
- Lowered levels of 5-HIAA (a metabolite of serotonin) have been found in impulsive and aggressive patients
- ASPD appears to be genetically related to alcoholism, and is frequently complicated by this illness
- Attention-Deficit/Hyperactivity Disorder (**ADHD**)

Psychosocial: Several factors in childhood are thought to be etiologically significant in the development of ASPD:

- Frequent moves, losses, family break-ups; large families
- Poverty, urban setting, poorly regulated schooling
- Little emphasis on communication; language was used as a tool with which to manipulate others, not express feelings
- **Enuresis**, **firesetting** and **cruelty to animals** are particularly strong indicators of future ASPD

Parents who are neglectful, harsh, physically abusive or substance-dependent make a large impact. Often, patients with ASPD were victims themselves. A family history readily reveals physical/sexual/emotional abuse, often with a substance-abusing caregiver. Frequent parental characteristics are:

- Mother: weak, depressive, masochistic, somatizing
- Father: explosive, sadistic, alcoholic, criminal history

By blending genetic and psychosocial factors, etiologic factors indicate that children with a high degree of aggression, who are difficult to calm down, comfort, and love are more prone to develop ASPD. Children learn that in an environment lacking consistent discipline, consequences can be avoided by seducing or bullying others.

Epidemiology

Estimates of the prevalence of ASPD are in the range of 3% for men and 1% for women. The prevalence can be up to 75% for incarcerated individuals. There is a gender difference in that men are more frequently diagnosed with ASPD, while women are more frequently diagnosed with BPD.

Differential Diagnosis

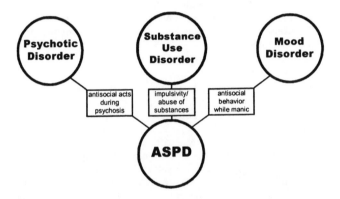

Mental Status Examination

- **Appearance:** Stereotypically have long hair, open shirt, jewelry, scars, tattoos, tight-fitting pants with large belt buckles, boots; mesomorphic build (bodybuilder); females may have heavy make-up; tight-fitting or revealing clothing
- **Behavior:** Strutting walk and erect posture; use space around them as if trying to impress; move closer when trying to manipulate; move forcefully; strong handshake; often casually slump down in chair with knees apart
- **Cooperation:** Varies with degree of interviewer's interest — ranges from highly engaging to quite hostile
- **Affect:** Expansive, cocky, hostile, irritable, shallow
- **Speech:** Exaggerated, vague, grammatical errors; glib, foul

language; malapropisms; "pseudo" sophisticated
- **Thought Content:** Grandiosity quite evident; past exploits are repeatedly emphasized; eventually get around to their agenda; blame the environment exclusively for their problems
- **Thought Form:** No characteristic abnormality
- **Perception:** If abnormalities are present, consider malingering
- **Insight & Judgment:** impaired, but can give "lip service" to what sounds morally decent; have great difficulty in seeing their deficits or contributions to problems
- **Suicide/Homicide:** More likely to be a risk to others than to themselves, but may emphasize suicide to manipulate for their agenda

Psychodynamic Aspects

The central dynamic in ASPD is an absence of conscience or a defective **superego**. Meaningful attachments to others are conspicuously lacking. People are seen only as objects over which to exert control. The harsh inner world of the antisocial is one of chaos, insecurity, and intolerance. Expressing ordinary emotions reveals weakness and vulnerability; only the extremes — blind rage or maniacal exhilaration — are experienced. Softer emotions expressed by others are actively devalued. Sociopathic patients exhibit a **primitive envy** and may seek to destroy what they most desire. For example, the victims of many serial killers were attractive women or members of happy, stable families. It may be that aggressive and sadistic acts stabilize their sense of self, and boost their self-esteem, which are again issues related to power.

Modeling parental **psychopathy** is another psychodynamic aspect. Parents may encourage demonstrations of power with repeated messages that life should pose no limits, thus leaving their children feeling entitled to exert dominance. Examples are parents who act with outrage at teachers, police, or counselors who try to set limits on their children. The term **superego lacunae** is used to describe the process where parents have their own problems with authority, and encourage this attitude in their children. It is "inherited" in terms of imitating parental behavior. A common denominator may be that after continual blows to their self-esteem, patients view the external world as barren and self-serving. They become predators, exerting power, and remorselessly justifying their disregard for the rights of others and the rules of society.

Psychodynamic Therapy

It is frequently stated that antisocial personalities are not treatable. At this time, there is no form of psychotherapy or pharmacotherapy that is consistently successful in reducing sociopathy. Everyone involved in providing "treatment" needs to make a decision about investing their time and talents in attempting to help antisocial personalities. To assist with this decision, a thorough assessment is critical. Some patients may be so damaged, dangerous, or determined to destroy the therapy that it is not possible to provide assistance. It may well be that these patients should not be accepted for treatment. Reasons for such a decision may be as follows:

- A history of serious assault, murder, sexual sadism, etc.
- Lack of remorse for a crime committed against an individual
- Obvious secondary gain for "being in treatment"
- Long periods of time spent in institutions or prison
- The inability to develop an emotional attachment
- Threatening to the therapist (overt or implied)
- Arousal of strong countertransference reactions

Source: Adapted from Gabbard (2000)

The diagnosis of ASPD encompasses a range of sociopathy. On one extreme is the predatory serial killer. The other end of the continuum consists of mildly sociopathic professionals who cheat on their spouses, leave debts unpaid, etc. The presence of some of the following factors is necessary for therapy to have a chance of succeeding: ego strength, an ability to express remorse, evidence of compassionate feelings, and at least one enduring attachment.

If a sufficient number of positive factors are present to justify starting therapy, the most important feature is incorruptibility of the therapist and the therapy. Convey this almost to the point of being inflexible. Any deviation will be experienced as a sadistic triumph, not gratitude for wavering from the boundaries of therapy. Anything that can be interpreted as a weakness will be seen as such. Sociopaths don't understand empathy; they see people only as interchangeable objects. Use unswerving honesty in outlining a therapeutic contract. Use direct language, keep promises, make good on penalties, and address reality. Antisocial patients project their cold and self-serving nature onto others. They try to discern what gain there is in being a therapist. You may have to admit to "selfishness" regarding your fees. Gratitude is not likely, but respect may be forthcoming for being scrupulous and tough-minded. Do not bend to their "special needs," regardless of the reasonableness of the explanation. At least initially, empathy can't be used therapeutically. Also, inviting the expression of feelings is not likely to be useful because of their deficient superego. Because of this, they are committed to act in order to feel strong and omnipotent. Restrict discussion to the possible outcomes of antisocial behavior, and focus interventions on confronting denial and minimization. Avoid emotional investment in patients or the progress of therapy. Show an independent strength verging on indifference. Progress occurs when words change from being used as manipulative tools to expressing feelings. Another positive indication is feeling pride at suppressing impulses. Despite the summary provided here, psychotherapy with ASPDs is fraught with difficulty and unlikely to be successful.

Group Therapy

Some institutions have reported gains in group therapy with inmates or inpatients. A frequent observation is that group members develop remarkable insight into the problems of others, but have a striking lack of insight into their own. A homogeneous group of ASPDs is the only indication for group therapy (hilariously demonstrated in the movie *Raising Arizona*). Even in inpatient educational groups, ASPDs mock authority, cause disturbances among other patients, and often try to lead a rebellion against the therapist.

Cognitive Therapy

Basic Cognitive Assumptions:
- Justification — "The end always justifies the means."
- Thinking is believing — "If I say it or feel it, it has to be right."
- Infallibility — "I always find a way to get away with it."
- Devaluation of others — "Other people don't matter."
- Denial of consequences — "I won't get caught."

Adapted from Beck, Freeman & Associates (1990)

Cognitive therapy involves a series of guided discussions, structured exercises, and behavioral experiments designed to give patients a more *prosocial* way of interacting with others.

Pharmacotherpy

An evaluation of DSM-IV-TR diagnostic criteria for treatable symptoms yields two potential areas for medications to be used: the reduction of impulsivity and angry outbursts. Most of the groups of psychiatric medication have been used to try to reduce these behavioral manifestations. SSRIs and mood stabilizers have been shown to have some success and are advantageous in that there is no risk of addiction. Other medications that have been reported to be of some use are: gabapentin, lamotrigine, verapamil, pericyazine, propranolol, buspirone, buproprion, and venlafaxine.

Course

Antisocial activity appears to peak in early adulthood and diminish with age. However, there is conflict over the degree to which it disappears. In general, the best predictor of future sociopathy is the extent to which it has already been present. Sociopathic behavior can be attenuated by social, economic, legal, medical, and interpersonal consequences. Long prison sentences, injuries, and financial and emotional bankruptcy later in life can have an impact on the course of this condition.

Chapter 7.
The Borderline
Personality

In the DSM-IV-TR, borderline personality disorder (BPD) is characterized by mood instability, unstable self image, and impulsivity. The word *borderline* refers to the "border" between neurosis and psychosis. Borderline personalities were initially thought to suffer from an atypical form of schizophrenia. From its initial description as a subtype of schizophrenia, BPD has also been thought of as an atypical mood disorder.

Mnemonic for Diagnostic Criteria — "I RAISED A PAIN"

Identity disturbance

Relationships are unstable
Abandonment is frantically avoided
Impulsivity
Suicidal gestures are made (attempts, threats, self-mutilation)
Emptiness is a description of their inner selves
Dissociative symptoms

Affective instability

Paranoid ideation
Anger is poorly controlled
Idealization of others, followed by devaluation
Negativistic — undermine their efforts and those of others

Movie Examples
- *Fatal Attraction* (Alex Forrest)
- *Malicious* (Melissa Nelson)
- *Single White Female* (Hedra "Hedy" Carlson)
- *The Crush* (Adrian Forrester)

BPD in the Movies
A common formula for cinematic portrayals of BPD is as follows: The borderline character, usually a woman, is attractive, talented, and alone. She makes herself available to a man who

seems interested but is unavailable to her (because of a long-standing relationship). In spite of this, she magnifies the interest or affection shown to her, and uses increasingly dramatic means (often sexual) to win him over. To spice up the plot, he capitulates but tries to limit her expectations by reminding her that he's involved. She ignores this and becomes distraught at the idea of losing him, believing that he really does love her. Her actions become increasingly frantic until some violent intervention is necessary to stop the continual phone calls, visits, threats, etc.

Interview Considerations

Borderline patients are often verbal, and it is not usually difficult to initiate an interview. They may even interrupt introductions to begin talking about something that is upsetting them. A formidable obstacle in interviews is the intensity of affect expressed by borderline patients. They are often in a state of turmoil and express anger readily. These patients demonstrate sudden and dramatic mood swings. At a given point in time, patients may be grateful for any effort to understand them, only to devalue it shortly afterwards. While the content of the interview may be distressing to patients, they also respond to internal cues that leave interviewers bewildered about the cause of the affective lability.

Borderline patients present unique difficulties because of their arsenal of primitive defenses and potent anger (often aimed at the interviewer). Authority figures are perceived either as providing total gratification (**idealization**) or complete deprivation (**devaluation**). Abrupt changes occur between these two perceptions. This oscillation occurs when patients receive something they are seeking (medication, admission, sick leave, etc.), or when they are denied these requests.

To maintain rapport, interviewers need to recognize that borderline patients interact with everyone in this way, and shouldn't take these difficulties personally. Acknowledging instability as an issue for further exploration may help sustain the interview. Redirection to clinically relevant material and simply hearing patients out can be helpful. Borderline patients can develop **micropsychotic episodes** under stressful situations and display features such as hallucinations, delusions (particularly paranoid), and loosening of associations.

Borderline Themes
- Chaotic childhood
- Parental neglect and abuse
- Impulsivity
- Disrupted education
- Legal difficulties
- Substance abuse
- Sexual abuse; early onset of sexual activity; promiscuity
- Frequent suicidal ideation or gestures
- Fears of abandonment; maintenance of self-destructive relationships

Etiology
Biological: BPD may have a genetic contribution. Studies have found familial tendencies towards poor regulation of mood and impulses. BPD patients may be temperamentally aggressive and have intense attachment needs. Low serotonin levels have been found in individuals who have been aggressive (both to themselves or others). Dysfunction in serotonin regulation has been well established as an etiologic factor in mood disorders. Additionally, dopamine seems to facilitate aggression, and is the major neurotransmitter system implicated in psychosis. It has been proposed that dysregulation of either or both systems may provide a neurobiological mechanism for some of the features of BPD. Another theory implicates a lowered threshold for excitability in the limbic system.

Psychosocial: The adage that "borderlines are made, not born" rings particularly true when virtual carbon copies can be made of borderline patients' personal histories. While not universal, there is an uncanny similarity in the family and social situations of many patients. Development is thought to be interrupted at Mahler's **rapprochement subphase of separation-individuation**. Between sixteen and thirty months of age, children begin to explore the world around them as a person separate from mother. They venture away from caregivers cautiously, returning readily for reassurance and security. Caregivers who interpret the child's return as an indication of a desire not to be autonomous will squash future attempts to explore the world. Similarly, caregivers who have pathologically strong desires to be loved and needed may engender strong separation fears in their children. Borderline patients can be viewed as constantly reliving this struggle with autonomy. They do not develop **object constancy**, and fear that attempts to separate will result in the disappearance of caregivers, leading to abandonment and the possible disintegration of themselves. This can result in such children being unduly intolerant of being alone and more difficult to parent. The initial provision, and later frustration, of attachment causes children to seek maternal substitutes. The first **transitional object** often takes the form of a cuddly toy, usually a stuffed animal. It is a common sight on inpatient psychiatry units to see adults bringing in stuffed animals to comfort them during their admission.

Disturbed parent-child relationships cause particular difficulty in the handling of anger. Children who later go onto develop BPD may sense that the expression of anger has a destructive potential, and instead deal with it by **splitting** it off or through **dissociation**. Severe childhood trauma is also highly correlated with adult BPD. This is most often present in the form of emotional, physical, and especially sexual, abuse. These devastating occurrences overwhelm children to such a degree that the use primitive ego defenses is necessary to cope with the trauma. While a genetic component may be present, a more accurate etiologic understanding is that BPD is more likely "made" than "born." This is supported by the typical emergence of this disorder after accumulated developmental trauma, usually in late adolescence or early adulthood. Patients who have BPD at an early age usually exhibit a worsening in their symptoms as they get older.

Epidemiology

The prevalence is estimated to be approximately 3% of the general population. BPD is by far the most common personality disorder diagnosis made in clinical settings. Here, the prevalence can be as high as 10% on inpatient units and 20% in outpatient clinics. There is a gender difference, with women being diagnosed at least three times as often as men. This may also reflect cultural stereotypes in that men exhibiting the same symptomatology are likely to be diagnosed with an antisocial or narcissistic personality disorder.

Differential Diagnosis

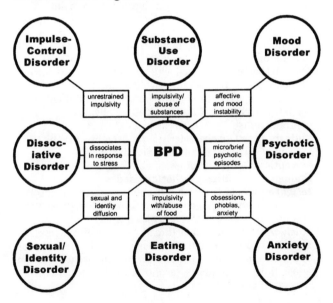

Mental Status Examination

- **Appearance:** May be dramatic; many prefer black — in clothing, hair color, nail polish, etc.; overabundance of eyeliner and excessive eyebrow plucking; pierced body parts (other than ears); tattoos; may have unusual hair styles — multiple lengths and colors; forearms, neck or other areas may have scars from slashing
- **Behavior:** Often sit cross-legged, curled up, sideways in the chair or on the floor (fetal position); may get up and pace due to agitation; in extreme cases patients can be violent towards property, themselves, or others
- **Cooperation:** Highly variable — ranges from ingratiating to hostile; will cooperate as long as interviewer remains sympathetic; can change abruptly to rage if denied requests or confronted about behaviors
- **Affect:** Intense and labile; ranges from seductive to outbursts of emotion (anger, tears, etc.)
- **Speech:** May be punctuated with epithets; otherwise normal
- **Thought Content:** Generally related to questions; spontaneous elaboration about interpersonal difficulties, themes of idealization and devaluation; obvious contradictions
- **Thought Form:** No characteristic abnormality; may be tangential, circumstantial, overinclusive, etc.
- **Perception:** Generally unremarkable; may have positive findings during **micropsychotic episodes**
- **Insight & Judgment:** Variable; depends on severity of disorder and current stressors; generally impaired; do not have the emotional distance to foresee consequences
- **Suicide/Homicide:** Suicidal threats, gestures, and attempts are a constant concern especially when faced with losses, stress or intoxication; can also be a factor in transference reactions and at times of therapist's vacations; violence towards others may occur during "rages"

Psychodynamic Aspects

Developmental fixation at the **rapprochement phase of**

separation-individuation leaves patients overwhelmingly preoccupied with issues of abandonment and separation. This leaves children feeling that because caregivers are not in sight, they cease to exist. Without object constancy, ambivalence cannot develop, as this requires simultaneously experiencing good and bad feelings towards others. This developmental arrest brings about an all-or-nothing reaction in children. When a parent is present, all is well with the world. When absent, the child feels abandoned. These dichotomous thought processes facilitate **splitting** as an ego defense to make sense of these experiences. In order to maintain this split view, patients **distort** their perception of events (sometimes profoundly) to restore equilibrium.

Factors pertinent to children (temperamental aggression, cognitive difficulties, etc.) or caregivers (over-involvement, neglect or abuse) can cause a pattern of increasingly negative experiences. Children develop predominantly negative introjects of themselves and others. They feel they are bad, the people they know are bad, and the world is bad.

Borderline patients continue their quest for attachment, and anyone who can provide a semblance of gratification is viewed with **primitive idealization**, in which unreasonable expectations are placed on such people. Because these unrealistic wishes are doomed to be disappointed, **primitive devaluation** invariably results.

Borderline patients have a low threshold for delaying action. Their feelings are expressed as a venomous rage, and their impulse is to destroy things (belongings, relationships, etc.). Normally, the ego delays the discharge of impulses and/or directs them towards healthy or socially appropriate outlets. However, borderline patients have difficulty sublimating their desires and modulating their feelings. **Acting out** is a term used to describe behaviors caused by an unconscious need to master the anxiety accompanying unacceptable wishes and feelings. In acting out, feelings of power replace those of helplessness.

Acting out also refers to behaviors relating to transference manifestations that have not yet reached awareness, or are too anxiety provoking to discuss (e.g. abandonment). Examples of acting out include exhibitionism, voyeurism, counterphobia, etc. What also happens frequently in BPD is **acting up** which is a conscious attempt to get attention, nurturing, sympathy, or other gains. Borderline patients have a poorly developed sense of self (**ego boundaries**) known as **identity diffusion**. They have trouble knowing where they "end" and where others "begin." This makes BPD patients especially impressionable and vulnerable to the influences around them. Helen Deutsch coined the term **'as if' personality** to describe this observation, which is reflected in DSM-IV-TR criteria three and seven. Patients live their lives "as if" they were someone else.

Psychodynamic Therapy

Increasingly, entire textbooks are being written to describe methods for treating borderline patients. Psychotherapy research continues to yield new approaches and new combinations of therapy. The psychotherapeutic treatment of BPD can be a most difficult, challenging, and ambitious task. It is a long and arduous process with no shortcuts.

Psychotherapy seeks to instill what temperament, upbringing, and numerous disappointing relationships have left patients without. The goal is to help patients emerge as integrated and dependable, and with enough self-esteem to value themselves and others.

Initially, patients are seen as requiring more "support" if they are lower functioning, and a more "interpretive" type of psychotherapy if they are stable and psychologically minded. This supposition has aroused controversy, although there is no particular formula or approach that works best for all borderline patients. What appears to be most helpful is a therapist who is flexible enough to employ techniques of a variety of approaches at appropriate times. Given the identity diffusion and instability characteristic of BPD, it is crucial to establish a "contract" for therapy that is consistently reinforced. Borderline patients have a poorly developed sense of self, and will, over time, benefit from this external structure. The details of the various parameters of therapy (fees, frequency of sessions, provision for emergency sessions, penalties for lateness, after-hour telephone calls, etc.) are less important than their consistent reinforcement. Therapists can choose limits according to their level of comfort, but two maxims in treating BPD are that:

• Boundary issues will be continually tested
• No amount of gratification will be sufficient; the more patients receive, the more they desire

Some patients react harshly to this structure and complain that they "came for help and all they got were rules." Working within rules is an important aspect of the therapy. Reinforcing boundary issues begins the process of dealing with patients as responsible adults. The therapist becomes the model for a self-respecting person who avoids becoming exploited, corrupted, or manipulated into gratifying patients' every whim. With time, therapists are required to act as a "container" for strong affects, particularly anger. Verbal barrages and venomous tirades will pervade sessions. At these times, patients are not in a frame of mind to ponder interpretations. These episodes must be endured and at a later time recalled in a way that will benefit patients. Two gains can be made during sessions such as these:

• The therapist's understanding of **splitting** helps patients to become aware that they see themselves and others only in polarized terms
• Patients incorporate the experience that expressing their "badness" does not destroy themselves, others, or the therapeutic relationship.

What makes therapy particularly difficult with borderline patients is their use of **projective identification**. Patients outwardly project a part of themselves that is unacceptable, while maintaining a link with it. The projected material is made to "fit" by unconscious pressures, inducing the projected emotional state in the therapist (like a self-fulfilling prophecy).

Handling anger in psychotherapy presents another major difficulty. Patients will insist that they are angry because the therapist is angry, but statements like these may serve to provoke therapists' anger. Borderline patients are exceedingly good at manipulating (unconsciously) their projections to make them fit the person on whom they are projected. This process can be very difficult to endure, and can cause marked countertransference reactions. Interpretations in such instances need to be made with the understanding that borderline patients do not have an observing ego. Simply telling patients that they are projecting their own anger seems to them like an attack.

Borderline patients are best suited for face-to-face therapy. This requires at least a moderate amount of activity on the therapist's part. Long periods of silence are difficult for borderline patients to endure, often fostering **regression** or other counterproductive reactions.

The other major difficulty in dealing with borderline patients is the propensity for **acting out**, particularly in the area of self-damaging behaviors. They often demonstrate a marked level of **denial** regarding the consequences of their acts. Interpretations that maintain a "here and now" focus, validate the person's feelings, but which also offer alternatives for further exploration, are particularly helpful. Such an approach is necessary because confrontation and the failure to achieve or maintain a therapeutic alliance are the two most common reasons patients terminate therapy.

Transference and Countertransference Reactions

Transference manifestations with borderline patients can be rough — rougher than even Rodney Dangerfield has it. Patients live out the unsolved struggles from their early development in therapy. Intimacy evokes fears of being engulfed or controlled by another person. Being separate from others is experienced as abandonment. These oscillations become the central dynamic in the therapeutic relationship. Patients can tolerate neither closeness nor distance. They have also been aptly referred to as **help-rejecting complainers** for frantically seeking and then discounting the attempts of others to help.

This upheaval manifests itself in the early stages of therapy. Patients initially idealize their therapists as rescuers and make their affections readily known, e.g. "You are the best doctor in this hospital. . . You are the only one who understands me. . I want you to look after me." Patients try to seduce idealized caregivers in a number of ways: emotionally, morally, sexually, etc. They give lavish presents, stop by for social reasons, etc. Very quickly, patients start to develop unrealistic notions and make unreasonable demands. A person who was once trustworthy is seen as completely so, until he or she disappoints the patient. At this point, this person is then viewed as completely untrustworthy with an accompanying extreme emotional response. This sets the stage for the inevitable devaluation, because no person can possibly meet these escalating demands. At this time, the devalued person is not treated just like someone who disappointed the patient, but "as if" he or she had ruined the patient's life.

Countertransference reactions can be just as strong. Borderline patients can exert an irresistible pull on therapists who respond by dissolving boundaries. Intimate relationships are started, sessions are extended and given more frequently, notes for absences from work are given, prescriptions are given for addictive medications, etc. Alternatively, therapists can respond by being unnecessarily punitive or sadistic. An awareness of these feelings is essential in dealing with borderline patients. Because of the uncanny fit of **projective identification**, therapists may have a difficult time sorting out where the patient's pathology ends and their own psychology begins.

Group Therapy
Groups allow borderline patients to diffuse their intense feelings

and direct them at more than one member. A group can provide a safe holding environment. It can offer, in a sense, a new family or a benevolent **transitional object** where **identification** and **introjection** can take place. This fosters increasing maturity and a diminution of the use of primitive defenses. Interpretations made on a group level may be better tolerated than those given in individual therapy. A group setting also allows patients to explore new ways of dealing with people in a protected environment. Because borderline patients lack a stable self-image, it is ideal to have group members who can provide positive role models. Such a group would contain a number of higher-functioning members with heterogeneous disorders.

Short-term inpatient groups can be successful when practical goals such as support, stabilization, and limiting regression are sought. A group consisting of recently discharged moderate-to-low functioning borderline patients is not likely to provide a therapeutic milieu.

Simultaneous participation in individual and group therapy, while not standard practice, supports patients through difficulties brought on by the group process. For example, confrontation or scapegoating by the group can be very anxiety provoking and discouraging.

A stable therapeutic figure helps patients contain emotions that might otherwise cause them to leave (e.g. feelings of deprivation or competition). Diluting transference manifestations between individual and group sessions can be a benefit for therapists.

Group therapy can also be difficult with borderline patients. Their direct expression of anger causes others to see them as unpredictable, offensive, and disloyal. This can effectively divide the members and this "split" can dominate the group. When this occurs, borderline patients are capable of **acting out** on this sense of rejection. Suicide attempts, personal attacks, and other forms of interpersonal sabotage may result and destabilize the group.

Cognitive Therapy

Basic Cognitive Distortions:

- Mistrust and suspiciousness — "The world is against me."
- Distorted perceptions — "People are deceptive and manipulative."
- Vulnerability — "I am powerless to control my life."
- Worthlessness — "I am unlovable."

Adapted from Beck, Freeman & Associates (1990)

The automatic thoughts in BPD create a vicious cycle for patients. Seeing the world as a malevolent place, they feel powerless to get by on their own strengths. They feel inherently unlovable and cannot turn to others. Convinced the world is out to get them, they have no sense of security and can tolerate neither autonomy nor dependence.

A key cognitive feature of BPD is called **dichotomous thinking**. The experience of people and events are distorted so they fit into only two categories — good or evil, love or hate, etc. Dichotomous thinking perpetuates patients' internal and external conflicts, magnifying their already low sense of efficacy and further decreasing motivation. Borderline patients can be difficult to engage in therapy. They lack the introspection and patience to participate in the **collaborative empiricism** needed for cognitive therapy. Cognitive approaches begin with modification of dichotomous thinking. This can be done by hypothetically assigning characteristics to people at both ends of the spectrum of a given quality, for example, reliability. A borderline patient will then go on to list impossibly high expectations for a reliable person and the embodiment of evil for an unreliable person. By then looking at real people in their lives, patients can begin to see that others can be mainly, mostly or usually reliable. As dichotomous thoughts decrease, control over impulsive behavior becomes possible.

Pharmacotherapy

While there is no definitive drug treatment for personality disorders, over ninety percent of borderline patients receive prescriptions. This illustrates the widespread overlap of borderline symptomatology with Axis I disorders, and the possibility of multiple diagnoses. However, other parameters that need to be considered. Doctors may prescribe medication when feeling pessimistic about psychotherapy. Patients in crisis may see a prescription as tangible proof (a **transitional object**) that a doctor cares about them. Some patients ensure that they get prescriptions by exaggerating their symptoms or seeing several doctors. It is prudent to prescribe medication for clearly defined target symptoms for a specific time period. Because of the risk of overdose, small amounts of medication should be given and, when faced with an option, the least toxic drug should be used (e.g. avoid **tricyclic antidepressants** (**TCAs**) if possible). Every major group of psychoactive medication can be used in ameliorating target symptoms:

Antidepressants: Patients frequently receive antidepressants, though studies have shown an unpredictable response.
• SSRIs have been found to decrease impulsivity and the frequency of self-harm. Some SSRIs have been indicated for control of bulimia. Additionally, they have a large margin of safety in overdose.
• MAOIs have been shown to be more effective than TCAs, but have dietary restrictions that must be followed to avoid hypertensive crises.

Mood Stabilizers: Lithium, valproate, and carbamazepine have been used primarily for episodic behavioral dyscontrol and reducing impulsivity.

Anxiolytics: These medications are frequently sought to "take the edge off" their mood symptoms. Benzodiazepines pose considerable addiction risks as well as potentially worsening impulse control through disinhibition.

Antipsychotics: Use of these medications for short-term control of psychosis and persecutory delusions is warranted. Additional benefit may be derived from the sedative effects.

Course

As children, borderline patients frequently had difficulties in school, particularly with concentration, and possibly had a learning disorder. Friendships may have been jeopardized or terminated because of behavioral dyscontrol, bringing about an early sense of social alienation.

In adolescence and early adulthood, the symptoms of the disorder flourish. Patients often do not complete their education or vocational training. With dissolution of their family of origin, or upon leaving home, they become involved in relationships that perpetuate and worsen their difficulties. Substance abuse is common, perhaps as a means of calming their intense feelings. The vast majority of patients diagnosed with BPD manifest consistent symptomatology over time. Some patients are re-diagnosed with other disorders, though other conditions can develop in addition to this personality disorder.

By late adolescence patients usually come to medical attention. Visits are frequently precipitated by disruptions in relationships. From this point on, BPD usually runs a rocky course punctuated with attempts at self-harm, hospital admissions, difficulties in relationships, and emotional instability. The consumption of health care resources can be enormous. Emergency room visits, with resuscitation and detoxification, in addition to hospitalization, demands for outpatient therapy and multiple prescription medications, all add to the cost. Added to this is the loss of productivity caused by sick days and other absences from work. The treatment of BPD is a long process that often requires hospital admission and crisis intervention.

Despite this pessimistic picture, BPD appears to lessen in severity within a decade of the first hospitalization. Several studies have documented higher levels of functioning and stability in jobs and relationships over this time. Despite the wear and tear on therapists in this first decade, it may be that patients incorporate something from each caregiver or hospital stay and integrate this over time.

Chapter 8.
The Narcissistic
Personality

The narcissistic personality disorder (NPD) was named after the character of Narcissus from Greek mythology. NPD is characterized by grandiosity, lack of empathy, and an unquenchable need for admiration.

Mnemonic for Diagnostic Criteria — "A FAME GAME"

Admiration is required in excessive amounts

Fantasizes about unlimited success, brilliance, beauty, etc.
Arrogant
Manipulative
Envious of others

Grandiose sense of self-importance
Associates with special people
Me first attitude
Empathy is lacking for others

Movie Examples
- *Groundhog Day* (Phil Connors)
- *Madame Bovary* (Emma Bovary)
- *The Fisher King* (Jack Lucas)
- *Wall Street* (Gordon Gekko)

NPD in the Movies
In a number of movies, narcissism is a personality flaw that the plot sets out to correct. The main character is too self-centered to see the detrimental effects that his or her actions have on others. Narcissistic characters take all of the time, attention, and resources they can get, robbing others of opportunities and even recognition for their assistance. Usually an intervention of heroic, divine, or supernatural proportions is needed to teach the narcissistic character a lesson that reforms his or her greed, pride, envy, exploitative nature, selfishness, or deficient social conscience.

Interview Considerations

Narcissistic patients, like other Cluster B personalities, revel in the attention they receive in interview situations. Especially in the opening few minutes when patients are given free reign to speak their mind, interviews go quite smoothly. Narcissistic patients "take the ball" and run with it quite well. Every nuance regarding their presenting complaint is related by them as essential information. Narcissistic patients like to surround themselves with "special" people. An interviewer paying undivided attention soon becomes the "best therapist in the hospital." The interview is used as an opportunity to reaffirm and enhance an already inflated sense of self-importance. Difficulties arise when the patient's grandiosity is confronted with reality. Patients can become hostile under such conditions and suffer a **narcissistic injury** even leading to a **narcissistic rage**. Responding with heated emotion, patients devalue interviewers for not having sufficient experience or intelligence to understand them. If this does not pass quickly, rapport can be re-established with appeals to patients' grandiosity:

- "It seems that others do not appreciate your abilities."
- "Tell me more about your accomplishments in this area."
- "You really seem to be headed somewhere."

Developing rapport with narcissistic patients can be difficult. Collusion with their idealized self-perception prevents a reality check, which impedes accurate and complete assessments. Even empathically addressing the interpersonal consequences of narcissism can detract from the interview because patients will feel threatened and embark on a mission to repair their self-esteem.

Narcissistic Themes

- Condescending attitude
- Readily blames others
- Dwells on observable assets
- Lack of empathy
- Hypersensitive to criticism
- Highly self-referential
- Exploits others for the gain they can provide for the patient
- Many fantasies, few accomplishments

Etiology

Biological: NPD does not appear to be genetically linked to other disorders. Temperamental factors may include a high level of energy, over-conscientiousness, increased sensitivity to unverbalized affect, or a lack of tolerance for the anxiety caused by aggressive drives.

Psychosocial: NPD has not been as extensively investigated as other personality disorders. This may be because narcissism is a component of several other personality disorders and NPD can be difficult to validate due to the subjective nature of the diagnostic criteria.

Kernberg views narcissism as a pathological process involving a psychic hunger or **oral rage**, caused by indifferent or spiteful parenting. However, some positive aspect of the child (e.g. a talent) or the environment may allow an escape from parental threats or indifference. This "specialness" facilitates a sense of grandiosity that blankets and splits off the real self which contains envy, fear, and deprivation. Kohut conceptualized narcissism not as a pathological deviation, but as an arrest in development. The seeds of NPD are sown when caregivers do not validate a child's needs, wishes, or responses. Many theories have postulated some form of parental deprivation, although empirical evidence is lacking for this view. Other theories posit that children who are treated specially, or at least differently than others, may develop NPD. Such children may be **narcissistic extensions** of their parents, and function to maintain esteem or as a replacement for something from their parent's life.

Epidemiology

Accurate estimates are lacking with prevalence estimated to be less than 1% of the population. In clinical populations, prevalence may be as high as 3%. There is a gender difference with men being diagnosed almost three times as often as women.

Differential Diagnosis

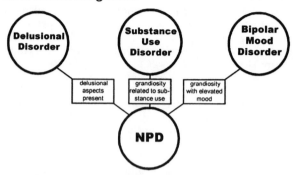

Mental Status Examination

- **Appearance:** Often immaculately groomed; may have expensive (or expensive-looking) jewelry and accessories
- **Behavior:** Often assume a rigid or authoritative posture; may caress their belongings or parts of their body
- **Cooperation:** Cooperative as long as interview proceeds according to their wishes or expectations
- **Affect:** Can range from withdrawn to animated; feelings are readily expressed and varied, but may seem "put on"
- **Speech:** Often well-modulated and articulate
- **Thought Content:** Related to grandiose sense of achievement, power, aspirations, connections and knowledge; can be notably derogatory towards others
- **Thought Form:** No characteristic abnormality; tend to overelaborate; may be tangential or circumstantial
- **Perception:** No characteristic abnormality
- **Insight & Judgment:** Impaired; are aware of others' poor treatment of them and of difficulties in relationships; react strongly when confronted with their own (realistic) contributions
- **Suicide/Homicide:** Consider in conjunction with Axis I disorders; not usually at risk, but this increases with a **narcissistic injury**

Psychodynamic Aspects

The DSM-IV-TR criteria describe the more flagrant behaviors and characteristics exhibited by narcissistic patients. Descriptions have been provided for "oblivious" and "hypersensitive" narcissists. This distinction is helpful in integrating the disparate views provided by two major contributors to NPD, Kohut (1971) and Kernberg (1975).

Kohut was a major contributor to **self psychology**. The term **selfobject** is used to refer to people who, while remaining external and separate (object), provide a source of gratification for the person (self). The soothing, affirming, and approving function of the selfobject persists throughout life though, in mature relationships, other people provide more than just gratification. In NPD, patients have a pathological need for selfobjects to help them maintain a cohesive sense of self. This need is so great that everything other people offer is "consumed" (**orality** or **oral rage**). This leaves narcissistic patients unable to develop relationships with others beyond this need. There is no capacity for empathy, sharing, or loving others. Narcissistic people function this way because they were treated in a similar manner by their caregivers. To a certain extent, all children become narcissistic extensions of their parents, which facilitates normal development through processes like **introjection** and **identification**.

Parents who are too invested in using children as **narcissistic extensions** transmit the sense that love is given for playing a role. Under such circumstances, children learn that gratification comes from others and from being "perfect" or fulfilling the expected role perfectly. The person's emotional reactions are not considered or reinforced as important. This facilitates a **false self** as the predominant manifestation in NPD. The evaluative process by which behavior is judged becomes **introjected**, and is experienced as criticism. Narcissistic patients are inwardly critical and constantly strive for perfection, which is also **projected** onto others who then are admonished for not living up to the patients' own standards. The internal world of NPD is also made up of the **real self**, which contains unconscious feelings that are denied expression. Patients feel empty, inferior, and fragile. Being a narcissistic extension causes feelings of deprivation and falseness to develop. Narcissists envy the success of others, and are particularly attuned to whether something will further their own cause. Innate aggression may explain why some narcissistic patients destroy the work, or good things, of others. Behavior in NPD is a defensive compensation for fragility. While dependent on others for their self-esteem, narcissists are vain, contemptuous, and "pseudo-self-sufficient." Expressions of gratitude are avoided to prevent an awareness of needing others.

Psychodynamic Therapy

Unlike patients with many of the other personality disorders, narcissistic patients often do present for help. They are aware that something goes awry in their relationships, but rarely see themselves as the common denominator. A typical situation involves a patient presenting in a dysphoric state, usually after a **narcissistic injury**. Therapy is often sought as a means to boost self-esteem. Several themes may be present in the initial meeting, with patients looking for a "qualified professional" (or the "department head") to:

• Listen to the minute details of the presenting complaint
• Collude with the devaluation of the other party/parties
• Reinforce that the patient did the "right thing"
• Assuage whatever guilt might be present
• Help patients to perfect themselves, rather than gaining an understanding of how they interact with others

Therapy with narcissistic patients presents difficulties. NPD involves a particularly defensive character structure that is reinforced by the way in which society views success. The traditional benchmarks of psychological health — being able to work and to love — may be difficult to set as therapeutic goals. Highly narcissistic individuals can do extremely well in certain occupations. They can find partners with personality structures that complement their own, and enjoy comfortable but emotionally compromised relationships. The goal in treating NPD is to help patients accept themselves without boosting their grandiosity or facilitating the devaluation of others. One of the difficulties encountered is that psychotherapy is a learning situation. Narcissistic patients often avoid novel situations that highlight their ignorance or deficiencies, preferring instead to be in environments where they have some status. Kohut and Kernberg are the major contributors to the contemporary understanding of the etiology and treatment of NPD. Since each approach has its own merits, an awareness of both enhances the flexibility with which NPD can be handled. McWilliams (1994) uses a plant analogy. Kohut's concept is a developmental one, in which a normally growing plant is deprived of sunlight and water. Kernberg's concept is a structural one, in which the plant has an aberrant part. Kohut theorized that parental empathic failures were the main cause of narcissism. Therapy centers on the repetition of this failed relationship in transference reactions such as the need for affirmation (**mirror transference**), idealization (**idealizing transference**), and imitating the therapist (**twinship transference**). Kohut emphasized the fragility of narcissistic patients and advocated a gentle approach:

- Taking therapeutic material at face value, preventing the message that what patients actually feel is different than what they express
- Taking responsibility when patients are feeling upset
- Avoiding what may be seen as criticism, stressing the positive aspect of experiences; highlighting progress when it is made

Kernberg views greed, and the devaluation of others, as defensive operations that require tactful confrontation and interpretation. Both positive and negative transference reactions are considered early on, with envy being a particular focus. A cognitive understanding is sought to show patients how their defenses prevent them from receiving help. Kohut's approach may work best with the "hypersensitive" narcissist, with Kernberg's being more suitable for the "oblivious" type. These approaches to therapy are not mutually exclusive. One approach may benefit certain patients at a given time, and with progress, the other becomes more valuable. Attention to transference, countertransference, and the effectiveness of trial interpretations will indicate which approach is more useful. Narcissistic patients are exquisitely sensitive to shame. A remark considered critical in early sessions (or at any point) can lead to termination. The gentle, accepting approach advocated by Kohut fosters a therapeutic alliance. Recognizing and admitting to imperfections not only avoids an empathic failure, but the patient internalizes a more realistic and humane attitude.

Pharmacotherapy

Narcissistic patients can experience mood swings that are influenced by their defensive structure. The dysphoria of a **narcissistic injury** frequently brings about requests for an antidepressant. Narcissistic patients are adept at persuading doctors to give them medications that may be ill-advised, especially benzodiazepines and opioids. They are vulnerable to hypochondriacal preoccupation and tolerate pain poorly.

Group Therapy

Convincing patients to participate is the main obstacle to group therapy. Often, the suggestion is seen as a rejection, or projected as the therapist being incapable of treating the patient. This process can be facilitated by beginning individual therapy first, and when the alliance is strong enough, continuing in a group format. Another recommendation involves simultaneous participation in both types, ideally with the same therapist. Each mode of therapy can complement the other, as narcissistic patients tend to run from their mistakes and hide from those who are aware of them. Narcissistic patients often dominate group settings, and take up a disproportionate amount of time. While they may enjoy the larger audience, the other members are soon resented for taking any of the group's attention. Narcissists rapidly seem to forget that they have any difficulties, and often take up the role of co-therapist. Their sense of entitlement makes them prone to transgress group rules, especially regarding contact with members outside of sessions. Limiting the group membership to one NPD can help minimize this. Narcissistic patients stir powerful transference feelings in group settings, and instigate considerable interaction. This can facilitate an active "here and now" confrontation.

Cognitive Therapy

Basic Cognitive Distortions:

- Self-Righteousness — "I did it correctly. I always do."
- Grandiosity — "Can you meet my standards?"
- Exploitation — "I'll find someone with better skills next time."

Cognitive therapy can be used to address three major features of NPD: grandiosity, hypersensitivity to criticism, and lack of empathy. Patients are encouraged to limit their comparisons to within themselves, not others. Enjoying activities is stressed, instead of focusing only on attaining goals — "I can enjoy ordinary things." **Systematic desensitization** can help lessen hypersensitivity to criticism. They can learn to control their emotional responses and look for positive elements — "other people can have helpful ideas." The failure to develop empathy may need to be overtly pointed out by asking about an awareness of the feelings of others. With role playing exercises, emphasis can be placed on how someone else might feel, not just react in a situation. Alternative ways of treating others is examined — "other people have feelings that are important too."

Course

NPD has often run a lengthy course by the time patients seek help. Narcissism may have certain advantages in early adulthood. It also imbues patients with the tendency to leave therapy. As a result, patients often do not engage in treatment until later in life. By this time, they have firmly established a pattern of using and discarding other people. NPD is frequently disguised under other complaints, usually physical or marital. Narcissistic patients do not easily forgive others or celebrate the successes of those around them.

Chapter 9.
The Avoidant
Personality

The avoidant personality disorder (APD) is characterized by inhibition, introversion, and anxiety in social situations. The DSM-IV-TR emphasizes hypersensitivity, fear of rejection, and feelings of inadequacy in addition to the avoidant behavior. The concept of APD has been criticized for having too much overlap with the schizoid personality disorder, despite their assignment to different clusters. The main distinction is that schizoid personalities do not desire close relationships; avoidant personalities do, but fear rejection.

Mnemonic for Diagnostic Criteria — "AURICLE"

Avoids activities
Unwilling to get involved
Restrained within relationships
Inhibited in interpersonal situations
Criticism is expected when in social situations
Lower than others (self view)
Embarrassment is the feared emotion

Movie Examples
- *Always* (Ted Baker)
- *Four Weddings and a Funeral* (Charles)
- *The Mask* (Stanley Ipkiss)
- *Zelig* (Leonard Zelig)

APD in the Movies
Passive, introverted, or isolated characters are not usually prime choices for lead roles in movies. Directors only have a limited number of scenes to help viewers familiarize themselves with the main characters. If something active or interesting isn't happening, this task is compounded. Possibly the most typical role for avoidant characters is that of the reluctant hero — someone with many fine personal qualities who just needs the right person or situation to help get started. Avoidant characters need a shot of courage, an enabling pep talk, an understanding romantic partner, or some crisis to get them off the sidelines.

Interview Considerations

Avoidant patients may or may not pose difficulties in interview situations. When some notion of a "guarantee" of acceptance is given, they become more amenable to sharing information and emotional experiences. Such a degree of acceptance is usually present to a greater degree in clinical situations than social situations. Patients may be quite open in interviews, making it difficult to gauge the degree to which avoidant behavior is present in social circumstances.

Empathic acceptance of patients' sensitivity and past suffering generates rapport. Once a sense of trust and a protective atmosphere is established, the interview will proceed readily. A detailed history of various emotional traumas often ensues. Patients frequently express feelings of being ashamed about many aspects of their lives. In order to maintain momentum in the interview, it is important not to trivialize these experiences, even if the patients see them as being "silly." Doing so will result in a retreat that reduces the effectiveness of the interview, though the usual avoidant behaviors will become more apparent if this occurs.

Some patients are extremely sensitive and anxious when interviewed. Unfamiliarity with clinical situations or past upsetting experiences may encourage their reluctance. Again, while the content of the interview suffers, the process provides valuable information. Under such circumstances, it may be possible to gather only essential information, deferring the details until rapport has been established.

Avoidant Themes

- Feelings of being defective
- Low tolerance for dysphoria
- Hypersensitivity to criticism
- Shyness
- Fear of rejection
- Exaggeration of risks
- Unduly set back by minor failures or disappointments
- Can become intimate with those who pass the test for safety
- Outwardly appear awkward; inwardly are hypersensitive

Epidemiology

Prevalence is estimated to be less than 1% of the general population, with an equal frequency in men and women.

Etiology

Biological: APD does not have a clear genetic etiology. Studies of temperament have found some people have a predisposition to marked social avoidance when faced with unfamiliar situations. Introversion also has been found to be a hereditary factor.

Anxious and inhibited patients share some of the biological features of generalized anxiety disorder, particularly hyperarousal of the sympathetic nervous system. Tachycardia, pupillary dilation, and laryngeal tightness are common physical signs. Baseline levels of cortisol may also be abnormally high.

The hippocampus and limbic system may be involved in inhibiting behavioral responses. Cognitive processing abnormalities may be present, as evidenced by both decreased habituation and decreased flexibility when presented with novel situations.

Psychosocial: While shyness may have a genetic or constitutional origin, psychosocial factors mediate the extent to which it is expressed. Intuitively, it would seem that children who were belittled, criticized, or rejected by parents have decreased self-esteem resulting in social avoidance. As children grow, these experiences are reinforced by their peers, perpetuating self-criticism and avoidant behavior. Through the cognitive process of generalization, patients come to expect similar treatment from everyone.

Alternatively, children may find that timidity helps manage raging impulses. Fears that expression of their anger can have destructive consequences lead to a pattern of avoidance. An awareness of situations where guilt, anger or embarrassment may be provoked, along with a strong and unpleasant emotional response, can promote avoidant behavior. As with the paranoid personality, avoidant traits can develop in response to having developmental handicaps such as sensory impairments or a disfiguring illness. There is a common thread between paranoid and avoidant reactions in that they share an alertness to the possibility of external threats. An equal emphasis on, or awareness of, personal limitations may modify emotional expression in these circumstances to produce avoidant rather than paranoid traits.

Differential Diagnosis

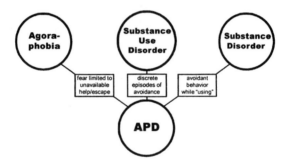

Mental Status Examination
- **Appearance:** None characteristic; typically are not concerned with latest fashions
- **Behavior:** May be anxious initially, with hand-wringing and agitation; may appear hypervigilant
- **Cooperation:** Cooperative in a receptive atmosphere
- **Affect:** Restricted/flat initially; wider range and animation seen as comfort increases
- **Speech:** No characteristic abnormality; restricted by anxiety
- **Thought Content:** Hypersensitive to surroundings; express anxiousness about relationships; may have ideas of reference
- **Thought Form:** No characteristic abnormality; may be

tangential, circumstantial, or vague
- **Perception:** No characteristic abnormality
- **Insight & Judgment:** Partial; are aware of anxiety and hypersensitivity; may have limited insight into avoidant behavior
- **Suicide/Homicide:** Increases in conjunction with an Axis I disorder; not generally a risk to themselves or others

Psychodynamic Aspects

The central dynamic in APD is that of shame, which involves a sense of not living up to an internal standard or **ego ideal**. It carries the connotation of being "bad," leaving feelings of impotence or helplessness. Guilt is the conviction of violating an internal rule (a prohibition of the superego) and a concern with punishment.

While a constitutional predisposition to feel shame may exist, it is reinforced and perpetuated through experience. Shame becomes a reaction within the first year of life and is especially evident during toilet training. Internalizing a variety of shameful experiences (e.g. emotionally expressive caregivers who are hostile or intolerant) leads to a diminished sense of self-esteem and a conviction of being "defective." Accompanying the low self-esteem is a sense of **dysphoria**, which develops not only from feeling rejected but also because of the sense of being defective.

Patients generalize their experience with critical and rejecting caregivers, and assume other people will react similarly. To avoidant patients, revealing anything of themselves leaves them vulnerable. They fear that should someone get to know them, their deficiencies will become obvious, bringing on criticism and ultimately rejection. The resulting dysphoria is especially hard to bear because, to an avoidant person, rejection appears justified. Avoiding potential harm from others becomes the central behavior in APD. Though patients have an awareness that relationships can be satisfying, they engage in social, emotional, and behavioral strategies to protect themselves. Patients even avoid thinking about things that may bring on dysphoria. They frequently find diversions to occupy their time. For example, television, movies, and live theater offer a semblance of human interaction while keeping them at an emotionally safe distance. These outlets facilitate another form of escape — wishful thinking and an active fantasy life. Avoidant people do not have enough faith in their abilities to bring about change, and hope that some event or relationship will appear as magically as it does in fictional works.

Psychodynamic Therapy

Avoidant patients are generally well-suited to the process of psychotherapy with a **supportive-expressive approach**. Initially, a supportive approach may encourage patients to take a closer look at the multitude of "escapes" they have developed over time. This is facilitated by empathizing with their sensitivity to social situations and their potent sense of rejection. With time, expressive approaches become possible when connections can be made between developmental experiences and their impact on current functioning.

As rapport develops, patients can be asked about the specifics of their reactions. This is especially helpful when done in a "here and now" manner with transference reactions. Patients can be encouraged to verbalize their feelings instead of avoiding them.

Pharmacotherapy

Because of the overlap with anxiety disorders, and the continual exposure to social situations, avoidant patients may require anxiolytics. Benzodiazepines are often sought because of their effectiveness and quick onset of action. However, their addiction potential and the chronicity of the difficulties encountered due to personality factors make these medications advisable for only a short time. Other medications are efficacious in alleviating anxiety:

- MAOIs have been used in anxiety disorders, with phenelzine being the best-studied member of this group.

- Tricyclic antidepressants, buspirone and beta-blockers may be useful.

Studies have consistently demonstrated the effectiveness of SSRIs in reducing anxiety symptoms. Research investigating the anxiolytic effects of newer antidepressants such as venlafaxine and paroxetine has been convincing. Medication can be used to reduce moderate-to-severe symptoms in order to help prepare patients for cognitive-behavioral interventions such as social skills training, relaxation training, and graded desensitization.

Group Therapy

Avoidant patients can be ideal group members and benefit considerably from this type of therapy. Much as in individual therapy, supportive approaches are necessary in the early stages. Therapists may need to be protective and see that patients are not pushed by the rest of the group. Overt encouragement will often be beneficial. Avoidant patients have difficulty speaking in public. When doing so, they are self-effacing and reluctant to involve others. These features can be directly addressed in a group setting. Secondary benefits, such as developing a more appropriate style of dress and an awareness of social trends, can help patients fit in more smoothly outside the group.

Cognitive Therapy

Basic Cognitive Distortions:

- Avoidance — "I am defective. How could anyone like me?"
- Rejection — "If someone rejects me, I must be inadequate."
- Criticism — "I'll never amount to anything."
- Misinterpretation — "If people think I'm useless, it must be true."
- Discounting praise — "Anyone who likes me doesn't know me."
- Catastrophizing dysphoria — "If I feel down, it will overwhelm me."

Adapted from Beck, Freeman & Associates (1990)

The effectiveness of any form of psychotherapy increases appreciably for avoidant patients if they confront actual (rather than imaginary) situations that cause them anxiety. This makes a combination of cognitive and behavioral therapy an ideal form of treatment for APD.

Patients demonstrate the same cognitive, emotional, and behavioral patterns towards the therapist as they do with others. Transference manifestations can be dealt with in a "here and now" manner in order to develop a working alliance. It takes considerable effort and perseverance to encourage avoidant patients to open up. They fear that when their reactions and behaviors are revealed, the therapist will no longer be interested in treating them. Only when patients feel comfortable enough to discuss their reactions to the therapist can the cognitions that pervade their daily existence be explored.

Cognitive therapy requires the recording of dysphoric thoughts and feelings. Patients actively avoid such experiences both between and during sessions. For this reason, an early intervention is to focus on the elements involved in the avoidant process. In order to do this, "**socratic questioning**" (**guided discovery**) can be used to have patients agree that in general, avoidant behavior will not help them achieve their goals.

Some of the behavioral techniques used in the treatment of anxiety disorders can be useful, especially **exposure therapy**. Patients first develop a hierarchy of threatening situations. This can be done either by using imagination (**systematic desensitization**) or real situations (**in vivo** or **role playing**). A list of predictions of the feared consequences is constructed for each situation. Generally, patients catastrophize the outcome, and observations made during the exposure supply evidence to contradict these predictions. In the treatment of phobias, **relaxation training** occurs prior to contact with the feared object. This may be beneficial for use in APD as well.

Course

Avoidant patients can also be conceptualized as being observers of life instead of participants. They lead their lives hoping and wishing for better, yet are harshly self-critical when they make a move to achieve their goals. While shyness can be adorable and even adaptive early in life, it becomes a serious impediment later in life when competition and assertiveness are rewarded. Avoidant patients often work below their level of ability. They have difficulty speaking in public, exercising authority, and delegating tasks — all qualities required for career advancement. APD is one of the conditions most amenable to therapeutic intervention. If patients can endure the initial relational difficulties in therapeutic situations, they can integrate their tolerance for dysphoria into a more assertive approach to relationships.

Chapter 10.
The Dependent
Personality

The dependent personality disorder (DPD) is characterized by submissive behavior and an excessive need for emotional support. Dependent behavior is particularly evident in borderline, avoidant, and histrionic personalities, as well as in mood and anxiety disorders. For this reason, DPD is often diagnosed in conjunction with other disorders.

Mnemonic for Diagnostic Criteria — "NEEDS PUSH"

Needy — has others assume responsibility for major life areas
Expression of disagreement with others is limited
Excessive need for nurturance and support
Decision making is difficult
Self-motivation is lacking

Preoccupied with fears of being left to care for self
Urgently seeks another relationship when a close one ends
Self-confidence lacking
Helpless when alone

Movie Examples
- *What About Bob?* (Bob Wiley)
- *Rocky* (Adrian)
- *Death Becomes Her* (Dr. Ernest Menville)

DPD in the Movies
- A talented or worthy person who initially refuses to take a chance on growth or independence and requires some event to propel him or her towards a more enriched life
- The devoted spouse/parent/friend of an evil character; their need to stay attached to these stronger figures overrides an appreciation for the unethical or immoral things being done
- Sidekicks for the main character; dependent personalities selflessly devote their lives to supporting others, don't mind missing out on their share of the credit for heroic deeds, and often do tedious work for their more flamboyant partner

Interview Considerations

Dependent patients are usually quite easy to interview. They readily respond when given attention and are cooperative. While anxiety may be an initial complicating factor, this can be assuaged through gentle persistence. Rapport is developed by showing empathy for their needs and by understanding how they have put their faith in others.

Open-ended questions are often answered appropriately, with elaboration on the details of their close relationships. Dependent patients are overly concerned with pleasing people. They are very attuned to the expressions and gestures of others. Because of this, they are quite malleable in interview situations. Patients can readily detect impatience if their answers to open-ended questions do not appear to satisfy the interviewer. They respond equally well to closed-ended questions and do not usually object to interruptions or changes in topics.

Difficulties can develop if patients get the sense they are not doing what is expected of them. Under such circumstances, they may give complete control to the "authority" of the interviewer. They resign themselves to answering questions, but may not contribute spontaneously. It is common for patients to form an immediate attachment with interviewers and to ask for advice and follow-up sessions. They may openly lament having to start over with someone new. Dependent patients are very sensitive about their submissiveness. They readily misconstrue exploration of this behavior as criticism and will frequently become tearful. Confrontation of any type frequently brings on tearfulness and pleas for help. For this reason, initial interviews can be more successful in looking for, rather than pointing out, dependent themes.

Dependent Themes

- Neediness
- Rarely live alone
- Subordinate themselves
- Work below their level of ability
- Continually seek advice
- Volunteer for unpleasant tasks

- May have a "somatic orientation," i.e. expressing their difficulties in terms of physical complaints rather than emotional pain

Etiology

Biological: Temperamental features consistent with DPD are submissiveness and low activity levels. There may be a stronger tendency for monozygotic twins to display dependent behavior than dizygotic twins, indicating that a genetic contribution may be operative.

Biological factors play a role in DPD. Children who are born with, or who develop serious illnesses, can regress and become dependent on caregivers. If the illness is of sufficient duration or severity, normal individuation may not occur. Because of the illness, autonomy is not encouraged, which becomes **egosyntonic** for everyone involved in the process.

Some studies have demonstrated an association between medical illness and premorbid dependent traits. Other findings have postulated a relationship between dependency and a general predisposition to disease. Dependent traits become more pronounced after the onset of serious illnesses and may be particularly common after head injuries where both judgment and physical capabilities are affected.

Psychosocial: There are studies to support experiences of both over and under-indulgence in the upbringing of dependent patients.

With respect to under-indulgence, prospective studies have found a higher incidence of dependent traits among children who come from impoverished backgrounds. Over-controlling caregivers and inhibition of emotional expression are common historical features seen in this model of DPD.

Children who are indulged by overbearing and overprotective parents can also develop dependency needs. Another feature of these families is criticism or punishment following attempts at autonomy. Children may fear their burgeoning independence will mean a loss of love from attachment figures. In this way, dependent parents who are over-invested in their children perpetuate the dependency they instill. The **oral phase** of development is considered the fixation point of dependent patients. The concept of orality is used to refer to the "hunger for attachment," rather than any reference to feeding habits. Additionally, DPD may be more common in the youngest child in a line of siblings.

Epidemiology

Estimates of the prevalence of DPD vary considerably among studies. In clinical populations it is diagnosed in approximately 3% of patients. There is a gender difference with women being diagnosed three times as often as men, though it is important to keep cultural and social factors in mind before making this diagnosis.

Differential Diagnosis

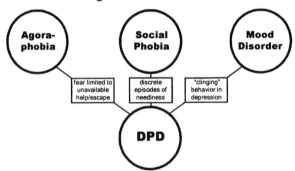

Mental Status Examination

• **Appearance:** May be less than stylish; often low esteem is reflected in dowdy or frumpy clothing; often baggy, neutral or bland colors; favor cozy or soft-feeling apparel

- **Behavior:** May be anxious towards a new or skeptical interviewer; behavior may include hand-wringing or tremor, holding own hands or an object for comfort
- **Cooperation:** Cooperative in a receptive atmosphere
- **Affect:** Usually demonstrate an appropriate range; a genuine sense of despair can be conveyed
- **Speech:** No characteristic finding; may reflect anxiety
- **Thought Content:** Passivity, letting others make decisions; express few opinions; egosyntonic reliance on others
- **Thought Form:** No characteristic abnormality; may be circumstantial, vague, or over-elaborate
- **Perception:** No characteristic abnormality; consider medical cause or substance abuse if findings are present
- **Insight & Judgment:** Partial; aware of dependence on others, but often do not consider it a problem; usually unaware of the extent to which their lives are hampered; do not wish to face or discuss dependency issues
- **Suicide/Homicide** Need to consider this in conjunction with any Axis I disorder; not generally a risk to others or themselves; risk increases with substance abuse, a general medical condition, or abandonment

Psychodynamic Aspects

Psychodynamic theories regarding dependent behavior emphasize a disturbance or fixation at the first stage of psychosexual development which is Freud's **oral phase**. Though this is now considered a somewhat antiquated concept, it still provides a useful framework.

At the beginning of the oral phase, the infant is in a passive-dependent relationship with the world. Gratification of oral needs, referred to as **oral erotism**, is achieved by being fed, and upon satiation, falling asleep. Later, when teeth develop, more aggressive features appear. Known as **oral sadism**, this phase is connected with biting, devouring, spitting, etc. The term **oral character** refers to adult analogues of these development stages. Oral characters depend on others to provide for them (as in DPD) or give them love and attention (as in NPD). In a sense, they want to be "fed," but demonstrate varying degrees of what it is they need from others, and what they are willing to give in return for this connectedness. Some psychoanalysts divided the oral character into a passive-dependent type (more consistent with DPD) and an active-dependent type (more consistent with HPD).

Though it may not be intuitively obvious, envy and jealousy are oral traits. Hostility and aggression often occur in dependent behavior:

- "You look after me."
- "You make the decisions."
- "You're in charge."
- "You tell me what to do."

This was recognized in the initial classification of dependent behavior as being a subtype of what was previously called a passive-aggressive disorder. Dependent behavior may be a compromise or a cover (**reaction formation**) for deeper aggressive impulses. Patients may earn "credits" through their services and use them to induce guilt. Other people are still "controlled" but by a more subtle and acceptable process.

It is also common to find over-controlling parents in the families of dependent patients. Much as in the development of BPD, attempts at autonomy were not reinforced and may have even been punished. A less dramatic variant could have involved rewarding dependent behavior. Another consistent feature is a low level of emotional expression in families. This may leave patients seeking overt demonstrations of affection, because verbal ones are not given.

Psychodynamic Therapy

Dependent patients are usually eager to get involved in psychotherapy. They ingratiate themselves by taking whatever is offered in terms of appointment times and frequency. They become model patients, rarely canceling appointments or arriving late. Therapists are treated with a sense of admiration bordering on awe. Regardless of the content of sessions, the process of therapy suits dependent patients' needs quite well. Having a strong, competent professional to turn to for understanding and support for an indefinite time period appears to be the answer in itself. **Idealization** in DPD is more subtle and enduring than that seen with other personality disorders, particularly BPD and NPD. Patients are tolerant of the lapses, oversights, and mistakes made by their therapists. As long as the continuity of therapy is not in question, such occurrences do not bring about the rage or anger that accompanies the **devaluation** seen in the Cluster B disorders.

The difficulty in psychotherapy is in conveying to patients that the goal must be to examine and alter dependent behavior, not indulge it. The therapist, like a catalyst in a chemical reaction, cannot be part of the final solution. In order to be successful, the therapeutic process needs to tactfully and empathically frustrate patients' wishes, and then explore the fantasies and antecedents of dependent behavior. This often takes place by denying requests for advice, extra sessions, or overt help with practical matters. Psychodynamic psychotherapy aims to uncover what is being masked by the continual search for a caretaker, and what frightens patients about independence.

In some cases, acknowledging progress invokes fears of separation and termination of therapy. Patients may begin to emphasize their difficulties, or actually regress in order to prolong the attachment to the therapist. A time-limited approach may help deal with this situation. If a certain number of sessions is agreed upon at the outset, the anxiety of termination can be discussed early in the therapy. This can also be used at a later point if progress is not being made. Some patients may not be able to tolerate breaking the attachment to their therapist and require indefinite, though infrequent, sessions.

Pharmacotherapy

Dependent patients invoke a strong "pull" in their physicians to do something to help them. This, combined with a frequent mixture of mood, anxiety, and somatic complaints can result in patients receiving medication for their problems. Dependent patients are eager to please and will do things that may not be in their best interests in order to comply with the treatment prescribed for them. They often do not complain of side-effects, take medication for longer time periods than is advised, and become "dependent" either psychologically or physically. Because dependent behavior can be a feature of many conditions, a careful diagnostic assessment is essential when it is the presenting symptom. Axis I disorders have specific pharmacologic treatments; there is no medication to cure dependent personality traits. Still, dependent patients receive prescriptions either as a result of their own initiative or their physician's. Overall, dependent patients may benefit from a trial of medication if they are particularly symptomatic, or develop an Axis I condition that is a clear departure from their personality traits.

Group Therapy

Group therapy can be an excellent therapeutic modality for dependent patients. Some group members may gratify the dependent patient's wish for advice and sympathy. Other members will confront such yearnings and behaviors. This facilitates learning and gives patients encouragement to attempt more independent solutions. The group is an ideal place to experiment with new ways of interacting. Group therapy can also be a place for dependent patients to hide. By idealizing other members (and the therapist), they may become perennial favorites and remain in groups far longer than is advisable. Group membership should not be seen as the ultimate solution for social contact.

Cognitive Therapy
Basic Cognitive Distortions:
- "I am inadequate and helpless"
- "I can't handle things on my own."
- "I must find someone to care for me and protect me"
Adapted from Beck, Freeman & Associates (1990)

The structure and time-limited approach in cognitive therapy can be very helpful in DPD. A frequent misconception is that therapy tries to immediately bring about an independent existence. Patients are prone to **dichotomous thinking** — either they are entirely dependent, or entirely on their own. Autonomy with enduring emotional connections to others is a more encouraging goal for patients. Often, direct examination of dependent behaviors and attitudes overwhelms patients, who may be unaware that this is their main issue. By use of **guided discovery** and **socratic questioning**, patients become aware that assertiveness, problem solving, and effective decision making can benefit their lives.

The practical, directive approach in cognitive therapy may foster an early reliance on the therapist. Once patients are committed to therapy, setting limits is useful in helping them discover their desire to be looked after. For example, if the homework assignment is not done, or patients have nothing to contribute to the agenda, they should not be allowed to deflect the responsibility for the content of that session onto the therapist. The standard cognitive approach is to provide an agenda if the patient does not. However, in DPD, submissiveness accounts for a large part of their difficulties and patients need to be encouraged to participate. Setting goals with an increasing gradient of independence is an important intervention. In behavior therapy, these goals are addressed by using **graded exposure**, possibly with the direct involvement of the therapist.

Course

Dependent behaviors, while adaptive early in life, can cause serious limitations for adults. In some situations, dependent patients exist happily in a symbiotic relationship with someone who "needs to be needed." Psychotherapies can be effective once patients understand that the therapist is not there to solve their problems for them. When patients develop an awareness of the limitations caused by their dependence, and see that autonomy holds advantages for them, they can work successfully towards this goal.

Chapter 11.
The Obsessive-
Compulsive Personality

Hallmarks of the obsessive-compulsive personality disorder (OCPD) are rigidity, perfectionism, orderliness, indecisiveness, interpersonal control, and emotional constriction. OCPD is often confused with the similarly named obsessive compulsive disorder (OCD), which is classified on Axis I as an anxiety disorder. Though some of the early theories did not distinguish a personality style from this major clinical disorder, these conditions are quite distinct.

Mnemonic for Diagnostic Criteria — "PERFECTION"

Preoccupied with details, rules, plans, organization
Emotionally restricted
Reluctant to delegate tasks
Frugal
Excessively devoted to work
Controls others
Task completion hampered by perfectionism
Inflexible
Overconscientious about morals, ethics, values, etc.
Not able to discard belongings; hoards objects

Movie Examples
- *Dragnet* (Joe Friday)
- *Moby Dick* (Captain Ahab, the whale too)
- *Remains of the Day* (James Stevens)
- *Unstrung Heroes* (Sid Lidz)

OCPD in the Movies

Obsessive-compulsive characters, like narcissists, are often prime targets for having to learn that there is more to life. Frequent depictions are as harsh, mean-spirited control freaks such as domineering bosses or workaholic spouses. Often, some disaster or event occurs that causes the main character to have to adapt to a less absorbed lifestyle. There is usually an attractive member of the opposite sex supporting the change as well.

In other portrayals, an obsessive character is the "know it all" who saves the day with some important piece of information (that apparently takes a lifetime of studying to have at one's command).

Interview Considerations

Obsessive patients can be difficult to interview. They usually relate the history in a pedantic, circumstantial manner. In order for the presenting complaint to be understood, a myriad of other details leading up to the current situation are also given. Hearing patients out will usually bring them back to the issue at hand, but this can take time. Trying to narrow the focus can bring about a hostile reaction, as patients feel compelled to supply all possible information. Obsessive patients are very attuned to control issues and will try to dominate the interview.

A good deal of the history is related in a "news" as opposed to "weather" fashion. Events are explained in a detached, objective manner devoid of emotional flavor. However, pointing this out can be precarious. Patients pride themselves on their objectivity; asking about what they are experiencing emotionally may bring about only a blank stare. In some situations you may need to suggest or label expectable feelings for the patient to identify. If not, a detour such as the following may result:

Q: "What feelings did you have while speaking with your colleague?"
A: "It was my feeling that this person was incompetent. I could have done the job in a much more efficient manner."

It can be difficult to develop rapport with obsessive patients. Showing empathy for their suffering means that they have not solved their problems. It may be more productive to attempt to understand their "dilemma." Try to use patients' exact words when rephrasing and reflecting, or semantics may become the focus. Wait until the issues are clear before summarizing, as these patients tolerate interruptions poorly.

Obsessive Themes

- "Misses the forest for the trees"
- Humorless; lack spontaneity
- Emotional constriction
- Fixated on details
- Inflexibility
- Hoards things
- Indecisiveness
- Few leisure activities

Etiology

Biological: There is little information available describing possible genetic links or physiologic findings in OCPD. Research studies have not found a genetic link between OCD and OCPD.

Psychosocial: The classic etiology of OCPD is a difficulty arising during the **anal stage** of psychosexual development (roughly ages 1 to 3 years). As children approach the age of two, toilet training becomes a major focus of the interaction with parents. Here, the "production" part of a natural process is treated as something unpleasant by parents. Children that are indoctrinated into toilet training too early (before the rectal sphincter is physiologically mature), or too harshly, end up in a power struggle with caregivers.

This is often the first intrusion of socialization into the infant's otherwise unconstrained existence. Achieving continence involves submitting to parental expectations (on demand) and being judged on the outcome. When children fail at the task, overly ambitious or demanding parents evoke feelings of being bad and dirty. Issues of cleanliness, timeliness, stubbornness, and control can reasonably be seen as linked to this stage of development. Failing to produce on schedule, with an immediate perception of disappointment, arouses feelings of anger and aggression.

OCPD appears to be more common in the oldest child in a family, who may have had more responsibility than the younger ones. Lastly, cultural influences are etiologically significant. North American society, in particular, rewards independence, hard work, orderliness, and punctuality.

Epidemiology

The prevalence of OCPD is estimated to be 1% of the general population with a slightly higher figure for patient populations. There is a gender difference with men being diagnosed at least twice as often as women. This disorder is also found more frequently within professions requiring meticulous attention to detail and strict dedication to duty.

Differential Diagnosis

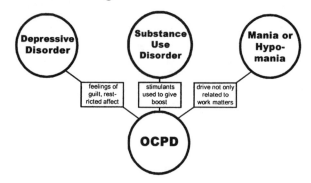

Mental Status Examination

- **Appearance:** Traditional clothing; "square" or "nerdish"; prim and proper; colors usually conservative; neatly groomed
- **Behavior:** Paucity of movement; body language not expressive; few gestures or facial expressions
- **Cooperation:** Often try to the control interview
- **Affect:** Low degree of variability; if expressed, often show anger or indignation
- **Speech:** Monotonous; lacks prosody and inflection
- **Thought Content:** Detailed description of events; need to tell the whole story in logical sequence; lacks emotional content
- **Thought Form:** No characteristic abnormality; often circumstantial, over-elaborate, or metaphorical
- **Perception:** No characteristic abnormality

- **Insight & Judgment:** Often limited; have difficulty in seeing the value of emotional life, or changing workaholic attitude
- **Suicide/Homicide:** Usually not a concern; however, breakdown of defenses with substance abuse, Axis I disorders, or a situational crisis can release feelings of rage

Psychodynamic Aspects

The central dynamic in an obsessive person is that of feeling like an unloved child. This may occur in reality, due to aloof and demanding parents, or can be due to the perception of this experience. Regardless, obsessive patients did not grow up feeling loved or wanted by their caregivers.

While the classical etiologic construct focused on the **anal stage**, it is highly likely that parents who were, or at least seemed to be, harsh and controlling would have been this way during all development stages. Being forced to "perform" during toilet training, and submit to other experiences engenders feelings of anger and fantasies of destruction. Parents who were unreasonably controlling squashed unacceptable behavior as well as the expression of anger and aggression. Attachment to caregivers is desired, though dependency needs remain unfulfilled. A psychodynamic understanding of OCPD involves the defensive handling of anger and dependency needs, both of which are consciously unacceptable to patients.

As children, obsessional patients were often praised for what they accomplished as opposed to who they were (i.e. loved for themselves). The child's behavior is then shaped according to that which receives the reward of parental approval. The notion of "being seen and not heard" is conveyed with the result that children behave like little robots. Feelings in general get relegated to the realm of weakness, guilt, shame, and being "bad." This leads to an over-investment in thinking, and rational or logical approaches. Patients are uncertain about what constitutes acceptable behavior. This leaves a strong sense of self-doubt, expressed later in life as ambivalence. Obsessive patients are notoriously indecisive, ruminating continuously to avoid making a wrong decision. Fleeting parental approval for "proper" behavior leads to the desire for permanent approval by being perfect. The demands of parents are incorporated as a harsh **superego**. Patients believe that by developing into a seamless, flawless, high-achiever, they will finally be loved and accepted. This leads obsessive patients to follow a series of hollow pursuits. They are driven beyond their own interests to succeed, but lack a genuine desire for the activity. The fuel for this fire is placation of the superego. There is a double irony in the relentless pursuit of these accomplishments. First, patients only get a transient increase in esteem, since the motivation for their achievements is to please others. Secondly, despite obsessive patients' apparent autonomy, they actually have little freedom from their superego, which is a persistent critic.

Patients fear "out of control" situations and seek to maintain control, both over themselves and others. Internally, compulsions undo or repent for an unconscious sense of having committed a crime (e.g. acts that would meet with parental disapproval and the aggressive feelings generated by the expected punishment). Externally, obsessive patients control their relationships because their unconscious dependency needs bring about fears that attachment to others may be tenuous. When patients were not able to control their past relationships, painful consequences were the result. Obsessive patients' libidinal wishes are punished as if they were crimes actually committed. For this reason, they may avoid situations where they might even think about life's baser elements. As a result, they may be overly moralistic and lacking in imagination. Rational thought, discipline, and orderliness bolster esteem which has been reduced by perpetual self-criticism.

Psychodynamic Therapy

One of the first challenges involved in treating OCPD is interesting the patient in therapy. Frequently, a crisis or loss needs to occur to cause enough emotional pain for patients to seek help. A lesser stress usually brings about their usual coping mechanism of working harder. Occasionally, patients will seek therapy to help with a specific decision. An "expert opinion" is sought to give concrete help with the choice, but not to explore the underlying ambivalence.

Control issues become evident in early sessions. Patients may devalue early observations and comments as being things that they already know. Other attempts at control may be seen in resistance to schedule appointments, or taking lengthy time periods to settle their account. An early difficulty involves the rambling, detailed descriptions of events brought to therapy. While frequently articulate, obsessive patients convey little to no emotion with their narrative accounts. This "droning on" actually serves to keep themselves, and others, in the thick of a smoke screen that covers feelings. This may be particularly evident when a strong affect threatens expression. Asking patients to focus on and describe their feelings helps tackle **intellectualization**.

There is a strong effort to become a "perfect" patient. Sessions will be attended on time and rarely cancelled. Patients will work very hard at bringing material they think interests the therapist. It is important to resist mechanistic explanations from patients by pointing out the difference between intellectual insight and emotional insight. A major therapeutic intervention involves getting patients to discuss their transference reactions. Frequently, these are reported as non-existent. It is crucial to pay attention to the last thing patients say before leaving, especially as they gather their belongings when the session is "off record." This has been referred to as an **exit line** and is characterized by heightened transference feelings.

Pharmacotherapy

OCPD is not altered by the medications that are effective in OCD. The neurochemical nature of the obsessions and compulsions are quite different in these two disorders. Patients with OCPD do not usually seek medication. Receiving a prescription feels to them like a reminder that they have a problem that they couldn't solve, which is a potent deterrent. Obsessive patients may also be very attuned to side-effects. They may be a "hard sell" and request to read a PDR (U.S.) or CPS (Canada) prior to accepting medication. Should side-effects impair or give the impression of impairing productivity, patients will stop the medication quickly. Benzodiazepines cause disinhibition in some patients. In crisis situations, the controls that keep anger in check may be lacking. A combination of alcohol and benzos, while always a bad idea, may be a particularly destructive combination in OCPD. Some compulsive behavior can be the result of an impulse-control disorder. Usually these conditions are treated pharmacologically with anticonvulsants, antidepressants, lithium, buspirone, or propranolol.

Group Therapy

Obsessive patients can benefit from group therapy and be valuable additions to the group membership. Their work ethic and reliability are qualities for other patients to model. Use of relatively mature ego defenses provokes less of a disturbance in the group process. Confrontation of long, detailed, obsessive explanations in a "here and now" fashion may be better tolerated in a group setting. Obsessive-compulsive patients can be encouraged to take risks and decrease indecision. Difficulties arise in groups when obsessive patients try to "fix" problems for others. A plethora of advice, suggestions, and plans are offered when other patients discuss their difficulties. Initially, little is offered to the group, as they wish to be seen as perfect patients. In order to satisfy their competitive urges, obsessive-compulsive patients will assume the role of co-therapist to try and assume some control in the group. This is often not resolved until this behavior is confronted by the group.

Cognitive Therapy
Basic Cognitive Distortions:
- "It must be perfect. I'll have to do it myself."
- "There is a right and wrong way to do everything."
- "If I don't control things, chaos will result."
- "I will dwell on this decision until I make the right choice."

Adapted from Beck, Freeman & Associates (1990)

The aim of cognitive therapy with OCPD is to explore the consequences of patients' automatic assumptions, and then alter them to facilitate a more realistic, humanist lifestyle. Selection of a goal, based on the presenting complaint, will have greater success if it involves the patient directly (e.g. "I'm never satisfied with my work" instead of "People around me don't work hard enough"). Examination of the **dysfunctional thought record** reveals themes involving the cognitive errors of dichotomous thinking, magnification, overgeneralization, and "I should" statements (Shapiro, 1965).

"I need to be perfect, or I am not worthy" (**central schema**) ➜
- I defer tasks to avoid failing
- I should be meticulous
- I must make the right choice

Each of these sequelae result from and reinforce the central schema. Another intervention is to construct behavioral experiments to test the validity of the cognitive distortions. A pitfall in this approach is that a cognitive solution is offered for a cognitive problem, reinforcing obsessive patients' tendency to look for tidy formulas and overly mechanistic explanations. Cognitive therapy strives to alter thinking and behavior; psychodynamic therapies reawaken emotions and allow them to guide thinking and behavior.

Course of OCPD

Obsessive patterns require considerable energy to maintain. It is common for patients to experience a mid-life depression when they become aware that their efforts will not achieve their idealistic goals. Friedman and Rosenman (1971) developed the concept of behavior patterns known as **Type A** and **Type B**. OCPD has considerable overlap with Type A behavior which is a risk factor for coronary artery disease. Obsessive patients are at risk for developing stress-related medical conditions and, in particular, psychosomatic illnesses because of their workaholic lifestyle.

References

American Psychiatric Association
Diagnostic and Statistical Manual of Mental Disorders, Fourth Edition, Text Revision
American Psychiatric Association, Arlington, VA, 2000

A. Beck, A. Freeman & Associates
Cognitive Therapy of Personality Disorders
The Guilford Press, New York, 1990

R. Campbell
Psychiatric Dictionary, Seventh Edition
Oxford University Press, New York, 1996

S. Chess & A. Thomas
Temperament in Clinical Practice
The Guilford Press, New York, 1995

M. Friedman and R.H. Rosenman
Type A Behavior Pattern: Its Association with Coronary Heart Disease
Ann. Clin. Res 3(6): p. 300 - 312, 1971

G. Gabbard
Psychodynamic Psychiatry in Clinical Practice: Third Edition
American Psychiatric Press, Inc., Arlington, VA, 2000

J. Kagan, J.S. Resnick, N. Snidman, J. Gibbons & M.O. Johnson
Childhood Derivatives of Inhibition and Lack of Inhibition to the Unfamiliar
Child Dev. 59: p. 1580 - 1589, 1988

O. Kernberg
Notes on Countertransference
J. of the American Psychoanalytic Assoc., 13: p.38 - 56, 1965

O. Kernberg
Borderline Conditions and Pathological Narcissism
Jason Aronson, New York, 1975

H. Kohut
The Analysis of Self: The Psychoanalytic Treatment of NPD
International Universities Press, New York, 1971

J.C. Loehlin
Are Personality Traits Differentially Heritable?
Behav. Genet. 12: p. 417 - 428, 1982

N. McWilliams
Psychoanalytic Diagnosis
The Guildford Press, New York, 1994

T. Millon with R.D. Davis
Disorders of Personality: DSM-IV and Beyond, 2nd Ed.
John Wiley and Sons, Inc., New York, 1996

J. Paris
Personality Disorders, Parasuicide & Culture
Transcultural Psychiatric Research Review 28: p. 25 - 39, 1991

D.J. Robinson
Disordered Personalities, Third Edition
Rapid Psychler Press, Port Huron, MI, 2003

B. Sadock & V. Sadock, Editors
Comprehensive Textbook of Psychiatry, Seventh Edition
Lippincott, Williams & Wilkins, Baltimore, Maryland, 2000

D. Shapiro
Neurotic Styles
Basic Books, New York, 1965

L.J. Siever & K.L. Davis
A Psychobiological Perspective on Personality Disorders
American Journal of Psychiatry 148(12): p. 1647 - 1658, 1991

S. Sigvardsson, M. Bohman & C.R. Cloninger
Structure and Stability of Childhood Personality: Prediction of Later Social Adjustment
J. Child Psychol. Psychiatry 28: p. 929 - 946, 1987

Index

The Author

Dave Robinson is a psychiatrist practicing in London, Ontario, Canada. His particular interests are consultation-liaison psychiatry, undergraduate and postgraduate education. He is a graduate of the University of Toronto Medical School and is a faculty member in the Department of Psychiatry at the University of Western Ontario in London, Canada.

The Artist

Brian Chapman is a resident of Manitoulin Island and Oakville, Ontario, Canada. He was born in Sussex, England and moved to Canada in 1957. Brian was formerly a Creative Director at Mediacom. He continues to freelance and is versatile in a wide range of media. He is a master of the caricature, and his talents are constantly in demand.

Rapid Psychler Press

Rapid Psychler Press was founded in 1994 with the aim of producing textbooks and resource materials that further the use of humor in mental health education. In addition to textbooks, Rapid Psychler Press specializes in producing 35mm slides, overhead transparencies, and digital images for presentations.